Normally associated with race day traffic, the Curragh Station in Ireland witnesses the embarkation of the Manchester Regiment after training on August 1914.

C000173576

£3 NETS.

RAILWAYS AT WAR

ALAN EARNSHAW

TRANSPORT

PUBLISHERS

COVER, TOP: *Bomb damage at Sunderland Station 1940.*

COVER CENTRE-LEFT: *Battle-bowlers on the footplate - see page 77.*

COVER, CENTRE-RIGHT: *Yellow train guard, see page 79.*

COVER, BOTTOM: *An armoured train of World War I, probably at Stratford Works.*

In the mire and mud of World War I, *possibly somewhere just to the rear of the Allied lines at Flanders, a Railway Pioneer detachment recover a Belgian 0-6-0 which had been derailed whilst in the employ of the Railway Operating Department.*

Published by
Atlantic Transport Publishers
Trevithick House • Penryn
Cornwall TR10 8HE

© TEXT: Alan Earnshaw, 1995

PHOTOS: as credited otherwise
Keystone Library.

Layout, design and reproduction:
Barnabus Design & Print
Truro, Cornwall

Printed and bound by
Booth Bookbinders Ltd,
Penryn, Cornwall

ISBN: 0 906899 48 6

CONTENTS

INTRODUCTION

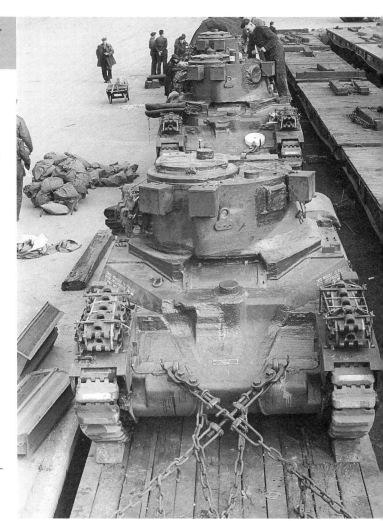

Until the release of the book Britain's Railways At War in 1989, the subject of how the railways coped in times of national emergency had been scantily covered in recent years. That first volume only touched the surface of the subject, although it did present a fascinating glimpse of our railways in the period 1939-45. In 1990 we followed up this subject with a similar introduction to the First World War. Neither of those books could, however, present anything near a complete picture of the role that the British railways played in the years of war. Though there is much still to be said about the subject of rail transportation in the two World Wars, this current publication is a compendium of the first two books, with additional information to set the scene prior to World War I, whilst at the same time examining the period between the wars. It also considers further areas of activity in World War II, in particular Dunkirk and D-Day. We also detail the post-war effects of the two periods - both of which witnessed dramatic changes to the British railway system, the first leading to the Grouping of the railways in 1923, the other to Nationalisation in 1948.

The Railways at War books were never designed to glorify war, so those who seek such entertainment perhaps need read no further. The reason for this stance is, because, from whatever standpoint you take, war is a dirty, dreadful business. It manifests brutality in otherwise normal men, results in untold squalor, suffering and death; in its wake it leaves widows, orphans, abject misery and massive national debt. Nevertheless this is an evocative subject, for the periods of war which have affected our country have a fascinating history. This is particularly so in the field of transport, when vast armies, their machinery and equipment had to be moved suddenly and expeditiously from one part of the country to another. Perhaps one of the earliest visual records of such movement is recorded in the Bayeux Tapestry, which shows King Harold's march from Stamford Bridge to Hastings in the Autumn of 1066.

Above: *From the 1840s onwards, it was recognised that railways might play a significant part in the prosecution of warfare, effectively delivering troops and their equipment hundreds of miles in a short time. For example, in 1846, 12,000 men of the Prussian 6th Army Corps were moved, together with their horses and equipment, in two days. Under conditions imposed by a forced march, the same journey would have previously taken three weeks. By the time the Second World War was in progress, railways and shipping lines would be moving men and equipment clear to the opposite side of the world. In this March 1943 view, ATC personnel prepare tanks for despatch to Russia.* ATLANTIC COLLECTION

Right: *Railways were also of great use for providing a means of taking battle weary troops to rest areas or on leave, and generally facilitating an easy means of repatriation from the front. For example, during World War II, a number of British servicemen who had endured the swampy ravages of the Burmese jungle were sent to the high, clean air of the Himalayas. My late father was one such person, being sent north of Darjeeling after the relief of his airfield at Imphal. Taken during his leave, this view shows one of the Darjeeling Himalayan trains that were exclusively used as leave trains during the period.* THE LATE JOHN EARNSHAW

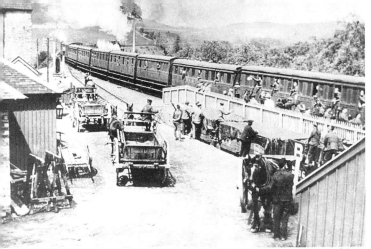

If railways were of benefit to move men away to war, they were also useful to repatriate the wounded and bring potentially hostile civilians or captured troops away from the front line and take them to internment or prisoner of war camps at the rear. During World War I a number of PoW camps were established alongside army training camps, an expedient measure which meant that troops in training or rest could serve to subdue the prisoners by their superior numbers. One example was found at Stobbs Camp in the Border country north of Hexham. Served by a small station on the NBR's Waverley line, our picture captures the scene where a military train, having brought in PoWs prepares to depart with fresh troops for France.
R.W. LYNN COLLECTION

Because of their tactical value, both as a means of advance and retreat, not to mention quarter-mastering, evacuation and repatriation of the wounded etc., railways were soon viewed as military objectives. In the American Civil War, Union forces became as adept at repairing railways as the Confederates had become in destroying them. A favoured trick by the 'rebels' was to set two trains heading towards each other on a single track at high speed, or a bridge or viaduct would be blown up and a train driven into the abyss below. In December 1916, German forces retreating south through Africa blew up the Ngeri-Ngeri Bridge on the line to Dar-Es-Salaam and drove all the stock into the gorge to prevent its capture by the British.
COURTESY THE TRUSTEES OF THE IMPERIAL WAR MUSEUM

All military campaigns, no matter how capable or superior the front line troops, must rely heavily on the receipt of sufficient supplies from the rear if they are to hold ground which has been taken - even more so if further advance is contemplated. Throughout history few armies without an efficient quartermaster corps and good supply lines have been able to sustain military objectives or advance, perhaps the most classic example being Napoleon's ill-fated advance on Moscow in 1812. The arrival of an early winter caught the 100,000 French troops unprepared and inadequately equipped, killing first the horses and then the famished soldiers. When the retreat was completed on 14 December, only 1,000 men of Napoleon's Grand Armé were fit for action. It was a classic example of an armed force over-extending the capability of its supply lines. A similar situation was witnessed, albeit on a much smaller scale, in the American Civil War. Towards the end of June 1863 Confederate forces tried to carry the war into the Northern Territories, culminating in the battle of Gettysburg (July 1st - 3rd). The Confederates lost 7,000 men in those three days, partially due to a delay in supplies coming up from Harpers Ferry over the Potomac River. Historians agree, it was this battle which changed the course of the war.

There are many other examples which could be quoted, but suffice it to say, military leaders and tacticians all round the world were beginning to examine ways of improving communications and supply routes, could the developing railways of the world provide the answer? As far as the English army was concerned, the problem of supply line failures had been at the back of many a general's mind, but it was the caution of Sir Arthur Wellesley (later Duke of Wellington) in the Peninsular War in not extending himself beyond what he could achieve which brought the matter to a head. Having allowed the French to escape, Wellesley was summoned back to Britain for a court-martial, but was exonerated and returned to the war with Napoleon. In 1815 Wellington was responsible for the final defeat of the French upstart at Waterloo and in 1819 he re-entered Parliament and became Prime-minister in 1828. Despite his numerous duties, Wellington remained convinced of the effectiveness of good supply lines, and throughout the formative years of the railways he took a keen interest in their military value if not their civic purpose. At the age of 76 he wrote a paper advocating the military potential of the railways in time of war, suggesting not only their value as a means of quartermastering, but also as a method of rapid advance.

Despite the 'Iron Duke's' faith in this form of warfare, it was not until 1860 that there were any positive moves towards its implementation in Britain. It was, however, quickly demonstrated by the second Boer War, that railways did have (or at least could have) a significant role in the new type of warfare that would emerge as the twentieth century drew near. The railways' value in international relief and rescue operations was clearly demonstrated in the combined international expeditionary force which was sent to quell the Boxer Rebellion in China (1900). The control of the railways led to the success enjoyed by the six-nation force, of which America, England and Germany were all a part. The military leaders were learning; what they saw both excited and frightened them. Accordingly, many nations began the planning for both the offensive and defensive use of railways in case of any times of future hostility.

Perhaps the greatest exponent of the military value of railways, at least in terms of promoting the concept, was General Count von Schlieffen, Chief of the German General Staff from 1892 to 1906. He recognised that Germany would probably have to engage in war with France and Russia, both of whom were likely to enlist Britain's support. The decisive theatre would be France, but as they could not possibly engage against France and Russia at the same time a defensive strategy would have to be evolved to deal with the threat to the east. Schlieffen's grand plan therefore called for the first advance to be against France, but if this was to be achieved without bringing allies to the French side, any such attack would have to be swift and decisive.

Realising that he could not make a front assault on France due to the heavy border fortifications, the plan called for a sharp scything movement through Belgium and into France through the soft flank of Flanders. Much of this depended on little resistance being received from the Belgians, whilst at the same time seizing complete control of the Est railway in France. Between May 1903 and October 1905, Schlieffen sent out an extensive number of spies to ascertain the strength of French and Belgium defences, along with others commissioned with the responsibility of gaining an extensive knowledge of the railway systems of France, Belgium, Holland and Luxembourg. Many of these spies actually obtained employment on the railway companies of those countries, others journied back and forth between Berlin and Paris posing as commercial travellers. When Schlieffen drew up his plan in December 1905, it is almost certain that he had an extensive knowledge of what lay between him and his objective. Much of Germany's gains, his report advocated, 'could be achieved by the capture of these railways, and the utilising of their rolling stock and locomotives to the service of the Kaiser'.

In principle the Schlieffen Plan should have been entirely feasible, but there was an unwillingness on the part of his successor Moltke to fully apply the plan, although a much modified version was put into practice in August 1914. However, as we shall see later, the Russians unexpectedly threw the grand scheme into disarray. Historians now agree that the biggest difficulty withSchlieffen's plan to use of the railways, was it inflexible intractability. The plan was an all or nothing gamble, and took little account of Wellington's philosophy of capture and consolidate, before continuing on to the next objective. Had it come off, Schlieffen may well have provided Moltke with the means to conquer Paris and thus France, but the rapid advance philosophy soon bogged down in a lengthy period of attrition which culminated in the stalemate of trench warfare! In theory however, the Grand Plan remained a major tactical consideration, even

As the 20th century progressed the military leaders recognised that whoever held superiority in the air, would also win the war. In many ways it offered a means of transporting men and equipment that was superior to that available through the railways, as evidenced by the adoption of parachute troops effectively employed by the Germans in Poland, Crete and so on. Even though it was not suitable for large scale movements or heavy loads, aerial power also had a further advantage in that it could be used in both an offensive and defensive capacity as well. Long before September 1939, British authorities recognised the power of the mighty German air-force, the Luftwaffe, and feared that strategic static targets may well be heavily attacked by their modern twin engined bombers. It was further feared that railways might become a principle target, as they had been during the Zeppelin raids of World War I, but strangely Hitler never adopted this tactic - seeking initially to concentrate on the Royal Air Force bases in the south of England and the Home Counties, before switching to the 'Blitz' of major towns and cities. However, the railway did not escape unscathed, and even small places like Whitby (pictured top) were badly damaged. Down south many lines were badly affected, with the station and engine shed at Newton Abbot in Devon being singled out for one vicious attack. Fortunately direct hits on engine sheds were the exception rather than the rule, although the picture bottom shows the result of a hit on the round-house at Fratton.
BOTH OFFICIAL VIEWS COURTESY DAVID JENKINSON COLLECTION

though by the start of World War II it was aircraft and not railways which were to form the means by which Germany would get round the static defence lines of her neighbouring countries.

In the few short pages of this book we can not possibly present a detailed history of all the railway events between 1914 and 1945, but we hope that it will provide a fascinating over-view of the role played by Britain's railways in the times of war. No conflict which involves the taking of human life should ever be glorified, but it is one which deserves covering in all its aspects - if only to show mankind the futility of it all. Accordingly, in this year of 1995, when Victory in Europe celebrates its

50th anniversary, it is fitting to look at how the railways were organised for, and coped with, war service. Of course, one has to temper the pride in the achievement of the railways under difficult circumstances, with the futility of war and the sheer idiocy of those who bring it about, but the record of the men and women who worked so hard on this part of the 'Home Front' is, I hope you will agree, certainly worth recalling.

Alan Earnshaw
Appleby, Cumbria
March 1995.

Left: *Direct hits on subterranean railways were thankfully rare, but on October 12th 1940 a bomb penetrated St. John's Wood Tunnel, which runs close to the surface near Marylebone Station. As a consequence, trains coming from the Aylesbury direction were terminated at Harrow on the Hill, where passengers transferred to the Metropolitan line services. The tunnel was quickly shored up and a timber framing inserted inside the bore to support the roof. This, however, prevented two lines of conventional tracks, so the Up and Down lines were interlaced with each other with relevant changes in the interlocking signalling to prevent two trains entering the tunnel at the same time. In late November an ex-GCR A5 class 4-6-2T passes through the timber framing, proving true the slogan of the day, 'the Railways Carried On'.* NATIONAL RAILWAY MUSEUM

Below: *On formerly quiet rural areas the likelihood of serious bomb damage was remote, but nevertheless railway personnel always had to be extremely vigilant. These activities were often coupled with Home Guard or ARP Warden duties, and an ever increasing daily workload as traffic grew more and more - particularly in formerly quiet rural lines. On a sunny September day in 1943, ex-GNR Class C12 4-4-2T No.4520 trundles bunker-first through East Anglia with the 3.40pm to Saffron Walden.* M. ELTHAM COLLECTION

The Boer War

The significant development of the use of railways to support British armies in times of war was first seen not in Europe (as had been envisaged by Wellington and Schlieffen), but in distant South Africa. As mentioned in the introduction, this came in the Boer Wars (there were actually two periods of conflict), which were fought between the British and independence-seeking descendents of Dutch settlers in South Africa. The first war took place in 1881, resulting in military and political victory for the Boers who sought the establishment of Afrikaner states free from the rule of British colonialism. However, it was in the second period of conflict, between October 1899 and May 1902, when the opposing sides made the most effective use of the railways. The first signs of the Boer conflict developing into a 'railway war' (as it was later described by Winston Churchill), came when the Transvaal Government closed the railway crossings over the River Vaal prohibiting goods traffic from the Cape, aiming to divert it on to the newly opened line between Pretoria and Delagoa Bay in Portuguese East Africa. With Britain threatening military force against Transvaal, President Krueger backed down and the border crossings were reopened. However, the 'peace' was an uneasy one and the unrest which followed eventually escalated and led to the mobilisation of 30,000 men in England plus the transfer of 10,000 more soldiers from British garrisons in India and the Mediterranean. This was to supplement the 10,000 existing troops in the Cape colonies who, it was estimated, were

In 1859, W.B. Adams (perhaps better known as the inventor of the railway fish-plate) wrote a paper entitled 'English Artillery Railways: A Cheap Defence Against Invasion' which, in part, stated 'If we look at the rail as part of an instrument of warfare, we shall be startled at the enormous means we have at hand, instantly available, from mercantile purposes, to convert to engines of war.' This paper came about as a consequence of a threat of invasion of Britain by France, and proposed the use of armoured trains for coastal defence purposes. Some forty years later the principle was fully applied in the South African campaign, when armoured trains were formed to protect long vulnerable lines of communication. One such train is viewed at Kimberley.

COURTESY SOUTH AFRICAN RAILWAYS.

initially out numbered six to one by the Boers. The mobilisation took place in Transvaal on Sept 28th 1899 followed four days later by the Orange Free State. The participants were ready and according to *The Times* the war began at teatime (5pm) on October 11th.

The Boers pressed ahead with the advantage of superior numbers, attacking along the route of the railway lines before the troopships could arrive from England. Moving south they took the various lines which crossed the Orange River into the Cape Midlands capturing the bridges at Norval's Point and Bethulie, the aim being the important junctions at De Aar, Naauwpoort and Stormberg Junction. To counter this the British poured troops up the Natal Railway from Durban and on the Western Railway from Cape Town but they were met by stiff resistance from well established enemy positions. By late October, the isolated British garrisons at Kimberley and Mafeking (on the Western Rly.) and Ladysmith (on the Natal Rly.) were all cut off and put under siege. The pattern was set, as the Boers (probably some of the finest irregular light cavalry ever formed) swept across the South African Veldt inflicting one defeat after another on the British. Early in November the Boers captured Colenso on the Natal line, cutting the railway and setting up a strategic defence line along the Tugela River.

In view of the success the Boers had made down the Natal Railway, it was decided to strengthen the British front line south of

Colenso thus creating a holding operation whilst the reinforcements due to arrive from England would be landed at Cape Town. However, on their arrival, they found the Cape province almost entirely unprotected and large numbers of troops had to be deployed to prevent any further excursions by the Boers on to the railway network in the Cape Midlands. In offensive terms, the general plan was to sweep the 1st Army north-eastwards along the railway, dividing forces at De Aar. One part of the army would continue along the Western Railway to relieve Kimberley, eventually pressing on to Mafeking (850 miles from Cape Town) where they would join up with forces coming down the railway from Rhodesia. The other section would travel east to Naauwpoort and join the Central Railway, up which they would proceed to capture Bloemfontain (the Free State capital) and Pretoria (the Transvaal capital). The role of receiving troops and supplies at the Cape then forwarding these on to the 'front' became the responsibility of Lieutenant-General Forestier-Walker. Yet, few of the British Generals had realised how mobile the Boer horsemen were, and even fewer still had realised that these untrained farmers would have the temerity to attack the supply lines causing considerable disruption to traffic and even more frustration to Forestier-Walker.

As the British forces pressed north, they met their first opposition at Belmont, just north of the Orange River. Completely outclassed by the

In preparation for the Boer War five armoured trains had been prepared at Cape Town and another one at Natal. Others were subsequently constructed, but their use was not fully understood by military leaders and the trains consequently suffered some significant difficulties. On the first night of the war one was wrecked by the Boers, two more were encircled at Ladysmith. At Chieveley, a train carrying young Winston Churchill was captured. However, the experiments with these trains proved effective, as Sir Percy Giraud said of this train, equipped with breach loading naval guns, at the Modder River: 'The gun behaved exceedingly well in every way. .... The experiments demonstrated the possibility of big guns being used in siege operations without any difficulty, the only limit to the size being the weight which the railway bridges will stand.' COURTESY SOUTH AFRICAN RAILWAYS.

Boers, and disadvantaged by a lack of cavalry, Lieutenant General Methuen's force suffered heavy casualties. The Boers then fell back on a succession of defensive positions and the British had to fight, with mounting heavy losses, all the way up to the Modder River. Despite the fact that Kimberley lay just a dozen miles away, further defeats at Magersfontein meant that Methuen's Army were to be denied relieving the garrison until February 15th. Even then, this relief was only achieved by leaving the line of the railway and striking eastwards and winning vital battles at Jacobsdal and Klip drift.

Towards the end of 1899 Major-General French had secured the small garrison at Naauwpoort Junction, freeing movement up the railway from Port Elizabeth and Port Alfred. Traffic from East London was, however, still pinned down by the Boers. Lieutenant-General Gatacre's humiliating defeat at Stormberg Junction on December 10th meant this strategically vital junction was to remain in Boer hands a further three months. With the enemy preventing progress beyond Stormberg and the Modder/Tugela rivers, the only line of advance

(for an army made up primarily of infantry brigades dependant on good supply route) was up the Central Railway. But, any advance north-east of Colesberg was blocked by the Boer forces defending the Orange River at Norval's Point. By the end of December, Britain had finally realised it was conducting something far greater than a punitive expedition against an uprising of farmers and settlers. Accordingly, a far greater mobilisation took place calling up militia and volunteer units from all over the country. To move the British offensive forward, command was given to Field Marshall Roberts and his forces moved against the Orange Free State in February 1900. Ladysmith was relieved on February 28th, though most of the Boers got away, some escaping by train to Johannesburg. On the Central Railway the army was pushing up to Norval's Point early in March and Bloemfontain fell on the 13th. The capture of the Free State capital was followed by the restoration of the railways in the state, allowing a push towards Pretoria. On May 16th the British finally reached Mafeking, some 220 miles north of Kimberley, thereby relieving the seven month

siege endured by Colonel Baden-Powell and his men. The capital of the Transvaal fell on June 5th but from thereon the war was to change its face.

Despite the loss of its capitals, the Boer movement continued its offensive through guerilla warfare, the Burghers attaching little significance to mere towns and cities which were 'just a collection of buildings'. The new commander of the Free State forces, General De Wet now insisted that the Boers exploit the main British weakness, the long supply lines leading from the south. With his Commandos raiding isolated British units and supply lines, significant delays were experienced in the prosecution of the campaign. The British had begun concentrating on the clearing of Boers from the line of the Natal Railway, allowing supplies to be moved up toward Johannesburg, but the resultant transfer of troops from the Central Railway led to numerous attacks there. During June the Boer forces split into three distinct groups, each one dividing into still smaller raiding parties, striking the railways at will. On June 6th Vredefort, Roodewal and the Rhenoster River were all attacked, with a supply depot at Roodewal manned by the Railway Pioneer Regiment being looted. After July all night running was suspended on the line between Bloemfontain and the Vaal, so great were the losses sustained in the raids. In August De Wet's forces were up in the East Transvaal, hampering British attempts to move east along the Delagoa Bay line. The hit and run tactics continued and by January 1901 the

The work of British railway companies supplying the means of taking men and equipment to their embarkation ports was substantial, with thousands of 'specials' being run. At the forefront of this traffic was the London & South Western Railway, who placed no less than 30 of its Beattie 0-6-0 goods engines at the disposal of the War Office. Many of these engines had been rebuilt in the early 1890s and were ideal for the traffic being conveyed from depots like Aldershot to Southampton.

LONDON & SOUTH WESTERN RLY. OFFICIAL PHOTO., COURTESY M. ELTHAM COLLECTION

British had been forced to suspend **all** night time railway operations in the conquered territories.

The reason for this was the fact that the protection of the British supply lines was very ineffective at first, principally relying on trenches and emplacements at vital points like bridges and stations, with mounted patrols between them. The inadequacies of this system were eventually resolved by Major Rice (Royal Engineers) who promulgated the construction of stone forts and easily erected corrugated-iron blockhouses along the railways at intervals varying from a mile and a half to 200 yards. The posts were connected to

The outbreak of the war, although tragic for a great many reasons, did bring some relief to the British ore mining industry, as the demand for lead and iron rose dramatically as the munition works and ordnance factories began a prodigious output throughout the United Kingdom. No less than 65,000 tons of lead shot was despatched to the British Small Arms factories alone. This meant a revival for the ore producing areas such as Leadhills in Scotland and Swaledale, Teesdale and Weardale in England. Up on the North Yorkshire Moors, the iron ore mines of Rosedale enjoyed a mini revival. The High Baring mines even benefited from the introduction of an electric generating plant for lighting, drilling and underground haulage - which, at the time was a remarkable and costly innovation at such a remote location. During the latter part of 1899 and throughout 1900, the North Eastern Railway lines serving these remote mining areas enjoyed a remarkable resurgence in traffic, and it was no doubt the increase in such traffic in England that spurred on the early completion of the Leadhills & Wanlockhead Light Railway. This view shows the Ingleby Incline of the Rosedale Railway, in 1900, down which the mineral ores descended from the plateau (where the mines were located) by means of a winding engine which can just be seen on the sky-line. AUTHOR'S COLLECTION.

The conditions of sick and wounded men in great numbers in overcrowded hospitals situated in or near the battle zone had long worried military doctors, particularly in the 19th century when it was clearly seen that despite advances in medical science, on average four men would die of sickness for each man killed in battle. For example, of the 95,000 to die in the Crimean War, no fewer than 70,000 were accounted for by complaints like typhus, cholera, scurvy and so on. To the Generals, the innovation of the railways presented a speedy means to evacuate wounded or sick soldiers from the front, and so was born the ambulance train. The earliest use of such transport being found in 1855 on the especially constructed railway which led seven or so miles from the front at Sebastapol to the base at Balaklava. The vehicles in which the wounded were carried were little more than contractor's trucks, but in the campaigns which followed the ambulance train fully evolved. For example after the Battle of Gettysburg (1863) 15,000 American soldiers were sent from field hospitals to Baltimore and New York in specially adapted coaches. By the time of the Boer War, significant developments had been made with regard to the provision of special ambulance trains, such as the Princess Christian which was provided by the British Red Cross and operated on the 3' 6" line out of Durban. Pictured below is one of the seven other Ambulance trains seen as it takes the wounded from the Battle of Colenso to hospital at Pietermaritzburg.
COURTESY SOUTH AFRICAN RAILWAYS `

each other by telephone and armoured trains ran regular patrols, but the manning of these posts along with similar defence posts at other strategic points (roads, river crossings etc.) tied up over 100,000 men at a time - roughly half of the British force. However, it was the system of 8,000 blockposts along 37,000 miles of railway which enabled the rounding up of many of the Boer Commando groups. Following capture the Boers were moved by rail to prisoner of war camps, with over 24,000 of the total number captured being shipped to POW camps in Bermuda, India and Ceylon. As the block-house system improved, the mobility of the Boers was impeded and as this had been their greatest asset in the previous years, their resolve crumbled. Sensing defeat, the leaders felt it was better to accept terms whilst

they still had some forces at their command, rather than wait for outright subjection. The terms were finally agreed and at 11.55pm on May 31st 1902 the Treaty of Vereeniging was signed and hostilities ended.

None of this details the role that the railway companies played in Britain, nor the way in which the Royal Engineers, the Railway Pioneers (and others) organised the transportation of men, equipment and supplies during the South African campaign. The subject is simply just too great to cover in four brief pages and will, in its own right, form the basis of a book I am presently writing on the subject. Suffice it to say that the subject has been included in this work, because of the influence that it would hold over both military and railway thinking in the two

World Wars that would follow it. This includes the major reforms which would sweep the British armed forces, and subsequently led to a restructuring of how quartermastering would be carried out in any future conflicts. Bearing in mind that military lessons were learned, particularly in the mobilisation and onward transmission of no less than 357,000 men to embarkation ports in Britain. Consequently, the railway companies at home also gained a great deal of experience, thus preparing them for what lay just 12 years ahead. Those experiences of the Boer Wars and subsequent reforms brought about in terms of mobilisation, transportation and deployment, would lead to Expeditionary Force of 1914 being 'the best trained, best organised and best equipped British Army that ever went forth to war.'

Road versus rail

Though we have not qualified it by demonstrating how vital British railways were during the Boer War, even that limited conflict was to demonstrate the absolute reliance which the country must place upon its railways in times of national emergency. Simply put, apart from coastwise shipping and canals, there was no alternative. The roads were simply not up to the job. In this instance we are not talking of local roads connecting town or city centres with the outer suburbs, nor of roads leading from one home counties' town to another, but of a national inland transport system capable of sustaining mass and rapid movement of men and equipment. There was no alternative to long distance travel. Connection between England and Scotland in particular was dependent on the railways or the sea. If a European war developed, the massive might of the German navy would automatically reduce coastwise shipping and transfer this on to the railways, particularly down the East Coast. On the west side it was a little better but the inland alternatives to rail were virtually nonexistent. For example, the road across Shap in the County of Westmorland (linking Kendal and Carlisle), was little more than an abysmal cart track climbing for long distances up hills with extreme gradients and precipitous drops. A horse-drawn cart running between Glasgow and Preston, might take anything up to a week to make the journey. Hardly a commendable means of commodious mass transportation in times of war.

So the railways were the only practical alternative, a fact the Government clearly recognised in a letter issued to the various 'Home Commanders' in April 1912. This communique stressed how vital the railways would be in times of hostility and emphasised the importance of ensuring that lines (particularly those on the eastern side of the country) were protected from enemy attack - specifically naval bombardment. Yet in its valuation of the railways, the Government failed to take notice of how this massive infrastructure had been created. It is significant to note, particularly in view of what followed both World Wars, that it was not Parliament who financed the main British transport networks such as the shipping lines and railway companies. Most were financed by private shareholders, individuals who invested large sums of hard-earned money which they had every right to expect a dividend upon - a dividend which could only result from good management, cost effective operation, and adequate responses to their competitors in the same market. It was such a philosophy that would provide the system upon which mass transportation could be delivered when England mobilised against Germany. Thereafter, this privately-financed system would also have to continue to sustain the country and her armies overseas throughout five years of war; only the railways could provide this means of addressing the transportation needs that were yet to come!

As an example of what the road conditions were like in rural parts of Britain immediately prior to World War I, we might take the isolated route over Shap in what was then the County of Cumberland. Today as cars crest the M6 at 70mph (and frequently much more), trains nearby achieve their summit at around 100mph by means of electric traction. Even so, weather still combines to defeat both means of transport at times, but one can not begin to imagine how difficult a journey it must have been in steam days when the climb by rail to the summit (pictured top) was not without its problems. A friend of mine (an old Tebay Guard) recalls that the railways were always concerned about runaways, because any wagons breaking loose on the Down road would run all the way from Shap to Lancaster before coming to a halt, unless otherwise impeded. Yet even this was far more reliable than the road which was virtually unmade. When one considers the type of vehicles employed on these roads, such as the steam lorry seen pictured below, unloading at Rowley Station in the nearby Pennines. Obviously there was then no real competition between road and rail.

AUTHOR'S COLLECTION (TOP) AND BEAMISH, NORTH OF ENGLAND OPEN AIR MUSEUM (BOTTOM).

Casualty of war. Having been involved in a side to side collision, an ROD Robinson 2-8-0, attached to Dunkirk depot lays on its side in the

Introduction to World War One

Noted historians have said that 'August 1914 was the month the world went mad', for the death and destruction which began that summer would shake the world to its foundations. An old order was coming to an end, and a new era dawned as political factions entered a crazy, downward spiral into what many considered an apocalyptic era. A global war which began amongst so called Christian nations, unleashed upon unsuspecting mankind a period of unbridled hostility as nation upon nation began to tear each other apart. New weapons of war were invented, and for the first time in a major conflict man took to the skies to satisfy his lust for carnage. It may seem harsh to pinpoint 1914 as the beginning of an eight decade period of major conflict, but since that time, as history shows, the world has seen little peace. True, there had been serious wars before 1914-18, but never had any embroiled the whole of the civilised world or involved such modern weaponry as to claim 13 million lives, so it can be rightly said that these events were a major turning point in the history of mankind.

It is therefore necessary to briefly summarise the political situation that caused the Great War, and note the major events which led to the British involvement. The origins can be traced back to the Franco-Prussian War of 1870, where Germany emerged as victors and under Bismarck began to enjoy national prosperity. In turn this lead to growth of German socialism, and although Bismarck tried to suppress the Social Democratic Party, it eventually swept to power in the national elections of November 1912. As early as 1909 Winston Churchill, had drawn attention to the growing tension in Germany, by stating 'Will the tension be relieved by moderation, or snapped by calculated violence?' He also envisaged that any such 'violence' might take the form of an adventure outside Germany, which might serve to distract Germans from their troubles at home.

Meanwhile, the Austro-Hungarian Empire was in constant danger of disintegration. The ruling Habsburg-Magyar dual dynasty was still in power, but the Empire was threatened by so many schisms from within there seemed the ever present threat of revolution. National-Socialists were in open alliance with Russia, and combined with disaffected Serbs, Slavs, and Moravians, the minority groups almost equalled

Within weeks of the declaration of war, almost every bill-board and hoarding in the land displayed posters calling men to arms. It was no different on railway advertising displays, as testified by the 10 recruiting banners on display at Liverpool in December 1914.
NATIONAL RAILWAY MUSEUM

the strength of the ruling powers. The only thing which prevented full-scale anarchy, was the fact that these dissident groups had not yet sufficiently settled their individual differences to pose a serious threat.

In Turkey, the situation was somewhat different, for their national aim was one of conquest and the creation of a Pan-Turkish Empire. This goal, they believed, could only be accomplished by removing what the Turks called the 'Russian despotism' in the surrounding Balkan nations. This aspiration was almost realised by the Russian Revolution of 1905, which set not only that country, but the whole of Europe into tumult. International monetary aid helped the Tsar recover his position, but the situation was still critical. In France the situation was also tense, and though

island Britain remained aloof from these entanglements, it too was preoccupied with civil unrest in the case of the Irish question.

The strange climax to these troubles began on June 14th 1914, at a time when at last peace seemed more assured. That day was the 14th wedding anniversary of Archduke Franz Ferdinand heir apparent to the Austro-Hungarian throne. As his wife Sophie Chotek was a mere countess, many regarded her as a poor choice, and she was never allowed to sit by his side on public occasions. However, as Inspector General of the Army, he was allowed to have his wife with him when he was acting in an official capacity at military reviews. So in desiring to spend his anniversary with his wife, he arranged to inspect his army in Bosnia. The review was to be held in the capital Sarajevo, but events of that day were to set the whole world ablaze. An assassination attempt had been plotted by six disaffected students from a local grammar school, aided and abetted by a Serb secret society who supplied the boys with crude weapons. During the drive into Sarajevo a bomb was thrown, and the infuriated Franz Ferdinand decided to drive straight out of the town. In the confusion one of the boys, Gavrilo Princip, stepped on the running board of the stationary car and shot the royal couple dead.

Many historians think this was the excuse the world powers had been seeking for so long, yet few of the military leaders wanted war, as they recognised it would cause an unprecedented holocaust. Indeed the Austrians had experienced serious trouble with the Serbs before, and had always been able to subdue them. Following Sarajevo they turned to their German allies for advice, who suggested that they take a firm hand with Serbia. The Austrians were reluctant to do anything hasty, but on July 23rd, they sent the Serbian Government an ultimatum designed to humiliate it. The terms were accepted by the Serbs, but not Russia who proclaimed itself 'protector of the Balkan States'. They stepped in, and threatened to mobilise against the Austro-Hungarian Empire. Such was the threat and counter-threat of European politics at that time, that it was anticipated that this would cause the respective parties to shrink back and thus ensure peace.

None of this bluff and bravado took into account what would actually happen if one country did mobilise, thus setting the long-prepared plans into motion. Previously mobilisation had been a long, drawn-out affair, but this was all changed to a matter of days by the involvement of the railways. In A.J.P. Taylor's book 'The First World War', it states that World War One was '.... the unexpected climax to the railway age', and further cites the escalation on the railways by stating, 'Railway timetables, cannot be improvised. Once started,

the wagons and carriages must roll remorselessly and inevitably forward to their predestined goal.' Basically, this is a simplistic view of the railway-based invasion plans which each country had drawn up in the latter part of the 19th century. The common saying of 1912-4 was 'Mobilisation means War', and perhaps this was a rightly held opinion in view of the Schlieffen plan, for once the railways began moving men and equipment towards the front, it would be hard to recall them. Even if a mobilised army was recalled to barracks, the movement would have been noted by the enemy, who in turn would mobilise his defence forces. Military escalation of the 1910s, evidenced by the movement of railway troops, was much a threat to the neighbouring nations as would be the action of scrambling nuclear bombers in the 1990s.

Eight decades ago Germany was convinced that the Russian mobilisation was sure to be slower than the French, and the Schlieffen plan was based on quick action in penetrating the enemy's defence. The railways were his means of accomplishing this and all the build-up was along the western border, unfortunately these plans were unexpectedly upset when the Russians mobilised in late July. On the 31st, Germany demanded their demobilisation within twelve hours or they would declare war, the

Russians refused and hostilities began on August 1st. Two days later Germany declared war on France and demanded free passage for its troops through Belgium. The Belgians refused and were invaded, an action which quickly brought Britain into the affray just three days later. All over Europe armies and reserve forces were rolling up to their allotted stations, and away went the trains to their prearranged destinations: taking with them an estimated six million men, who were deposited on the various sides of the battle-fields. The dogs of war were unleashed!

With Britain entering the war on August 5th 1914, a new era was set for the nation's railways and the people who worked thereon. In less than 90 years the railways had evolved from simple waggonways and plateways, to a highly organised national transport network, operated by independent companies and organised into a market-place where there was stiff commercial opposition from rival undertakings. For the first time since the opening of the Stockton & Darlington Railway in 1825, the railway companies would now have to work together in a harmonious display of national interests. Could the various factions be brought into a cohesive working partnership that would sustain the country's considerable transport needs in the desperate years ahead?

At a meeting of the War Cabinet in January 1917, instructions were given for the construction of a train-ferry service between England and France. Two English terminals were constructed, one at Richborough and one at Southampton, connecting the ports of Calais and dunkirk. The service did not start until February 10th 1918, when three identical ferries were commissioned. Each had a main train-deck which carried four sets of parallel lines, giving a total track length of 1,080 ft. This afforded the carriage of 54 standard wagons or the equivalent in coaches or locomotives. The vessels were twin screw with two sets of triple-expansion engines, and were capable of about 12 knots. They were provided with searchlights, wireless and anti-aircraft/submarine guns. A crew of 65 manned the vessels, but no passengers were carried.
THE TANK MUSEUM

The naval build-up was much slower than the army's, and many historians point to the fact that this was due to perpetual penny-pinching by successive governments. Whether this is an accurate overall picture or not, it is certainly true of the rail facilities connected with our maritime defence. There was a general shortage of the special rail wagons which were required to meet the Navy's unusual demands. As in the case of vehicles for conveying heavy guns: a few 'gun-sets' capable of carrying guns up to 100 tons were available but these were unlikely to be sufficient in a war. In the meanwhile, guns like the 56 ton example seen at Toton in 1906, had to be carried on an improvised 'gun-set' and is mounted on two MR armour-plate wagons (Nos. 116073 and 34842) Traction engine truck D333 and a 10-ton brake van complete the train.
NATIONAL RAILWAY MUSEUM

The engine that came back! Of all the railway equipment despatched to France, provision was made for expendable losses, allowing for enemy action. However, it was understood that the enemy must not be allowed to capture British equipment intact, and if this was likely, the equipment should be destroyed first. This was not the case with a Midland 0-6-0, No. 2717 which was captured by the Germans near Cambrai in 1917. After being put to use on German controlled lines, it was later re-captured and returned to the Midland Railway after the armistice.
NATIONAL RAILWAY MUSEUM

Preparation for War

The abiding memory of most participants in the mobilisation of August 1914, is the role the railways played, and the smooth running of the entire transport operations. What is not so widely known, are the extensive efforts put into the preparation of the mobilisation plans. In railway terms the origins of these could be traced back over fifty years. The American Civil War (1861-5) showed the effectiveness of rail transport in modern warfare, and it was in the Prussian State of Germany that there came the first planned system for the utilisation of railways in wartime. The idea spread through Europe, and soon each country had evolved plans for, if not actually formed, strategical railway troops. The basic concept was the formation of a construction corps, and a railway reserve. These trained railwaymen and engineers would follow the advancing army, taking control of, repairing, and operating captured railway systems to support further military advances.

In England the concept had been advanced by the Duke of Wellington as early as 1845, but it was not until 1860 that there came the proposal to form a railway reserve to act in support of coastal defences in the time of national emergency. Various reports were studied, but that by Charles Manby FRS was accepted, and in January 1865 the Engineer & Railway Volunteer Staff Corps was formed. Its purpose 'to direct the skilled labour and of railway transport to the purposes of national defence, and for the preparing, in time of peace, a system on which duties should be conducted'. It is interesting to note that such duties were strictly confined to the British Isles, and unlike all the other European countries, Britain did not envisage the need for 'occupationary railway troops'. This largely stemmed from the fact that Britain was an island, and it had no adjoining country which it might be forced to occupy. The result of this was to dog the Railway Reserve for

---

As the stern realities of the conflict in France became realised in the autumn of 1914, the public hope that 'the war would be over by Christmas' gradually disappeared. It was to be a war of attrition, and the winning of it would largely depend on the side with the best organisation for getting men and munitions to the Front. In February 1915 Lord Kitchener enlisted the assistance of the NER's Mr. Eric C. Geddes in speeding up the movement of munitions and other vital materials. Then on October 7th 1916 he was made Director-General of Military Railways and Deputy Quartermaster General (Transport), yet within just two weeks he was also appointed as Inspector General of Transport to the British Armies in France. In order for him to inspect the facilities under his control, a train of eight 6-wheeled coaches was placed at his disposal. The train is pictured here with an NER 2-4-2T No. 205, the baggage and store vans are marshalled at the front.
NATIONAL RAILWAY MUSEUM

many years, and ensured that (a) it was only ever a numerically small reserve, and (b) that Government spending was proportionally low.

The Corps was purely voluntary (until it became part of the Territorial Reserve 1907) and was initially staffed only by officers. Its members were contractors, civil engineers, railway and dock managers, and in some instances members of the Board of Trade. But in an emergency, the Corps figured it could rely on 12,000 to 20,000 men, mostly navvies. Its main work was drawing up the mobilisation timetables, by which the railways would speed men to the defence of the realm. Though establishing the Corps was a major step, the Government felt it needed to be able to control and coordinate the various railway, naval and military needs of a country at war. Therefore in 1896, the War Office created the Army Railway Council, which was comprised of two representatives of the Quarter-master General, six railway managers (four from England and one each from Ireland and Scotland), two members of the Corps, one BoT Inspector, one Mobilisation Officer, and two officers from the Admiralty.

The council's objectives were: (1) generally advise the Secretary of State for War on railway matters; (2) to arrange with all railway companies a detailed scheme in the event of mobilisation; (3) settle the number and composition of trains required to effect same; (4) to determine the best ways of communicating War Office needs to and from the railway companies; (5) to

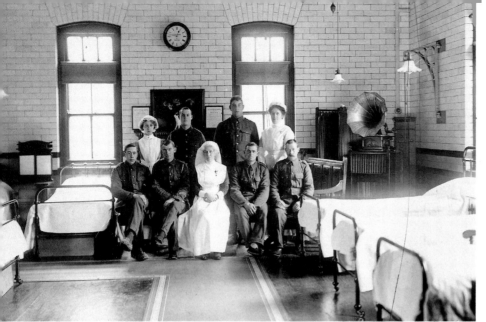

All manner of railway facilities were to be put at the disposal of the military, including the Cottage Hospital at the L&YR's Horwich Works, opened in 1895. A group of convalescing servicemen are pictured here with the sister in 1915, but note the 'ghetto-blaster' in the corner as evidence that even back then, hospital wards were not altogether the strict, quiet places we might imagine.
NATIONAL RAILWAY MUSEUM

determine the key stations where Railway Staff Officers would be located, and how they could act as intermediaries between the railways and the War Office; (6) to determine where extra sidings, platforms and loading facilities would be needed. The results of the council's objectives were not immediately evident, and indeed the full council only met four times between 1897 and 1910, but things were moving quietly ahead. The South African War and the Boxer Rebellion in China prompted the Government to look more closely at the needs of its railways in war, and in 1903 the name of the council was changed to War Railway Council – a title more in keeping with the wishes of the Lords of the Admiralty.

In 1903 the work of mobilisation timetables was taken up afresh, and although the various military powers were reluctant to supply such 'secret' data, the railway companies could not work without it. The debate was long and hard, but suffice it to say, that by compromise the information was supplied and the work was entrusted to a select few timetable experts. This mammoth task was undertaken with little or no remuneration, and the strain imposed by the work led to the early death of one noted expert. Meanwhile, a more strenuous debate went on about the formation of a pool of 4ft 8 $\frac{1}{2}$in gauge locomotives, rolling stock and workers, which the Council expected the railway companies to supply in the times of emergency overseas. The companies were reluctant to do this without sufficient compensation, but the Government took the view that its various colonial governments had agreed to supply 3ft 6in gauge stock at only nominal costs, and the companies should do likewise. There the matter remained dead-locked, but as war drew near the situation was amicably resolved as we will see later. Meanwhile on the 'home front', preparations went ahead – ostensibly for National Defence, though the far-sighted could see the developing role of the railways in times of aggression. In 1911 the country was divided into Commands, and for each area command, a secretary railway company was appointed to coordinate the needs of the military. These were:-

Eastern Command – South Eastern & Chatham;

Southern Command – London & South Western;
Western Command – LNWR;
North Command – North Eastern;
Scottish Command – North British;
Irish Command – Great Northern of Ireland.

Under the command system the mobilisation, which had previously been a relatively small matter, became an exceedingly serious concern.

From here-on in, the control of the railways in wartime assumed even greater significance, especially in view of the critical developments in international politics in 1911. It was yet to be resolved how the Government could control the railways in time of war, ensuring both the needs of the civil population and the demands of the War Office. Basically it had two options: (1) to employ section 16 of the Regulation of the Forces Act (1871), which would allow it to take over the complete running of the railways, as though under state control through military law; or, (2) to employ the National Defence Act of 1888, allowing the Government to demand individual companies to comply with its needs and wishes in time of emergency. Initially the latter Act seemed the most expedient, and in general, railway managers were extremely apprehensive about letting the state take control of the railways. Unfortunately, the second Act did not allow for any harmonious development of national railway services which would be needed in times of war. Indeed, the Government had very serious grounds for believing that delays would be occasioned to vital military traffic where one railway system met with another.

The real salvation finally came in a totally unexpected form, from a group which had been established to devise the strategy for provisioning London and the south east during times of war with continental Europe. This group was a sub-committee of the War Railway Council, and comprised of the general managers of the LNWR, GWR, LSWR, GNR, GCR and Midland. Under the chairmanship of Frank Ree (LNWR), the committee formulated its specified objectives, but added three recommendations which would at last resolve the issues of who controlled the railway when war eventually broke out. These were:- (1) Adoption of the 1871 Act,

The vast camp of the Lancashire Fusiliers near Turton & Edgeworth station, on the Bolton-Blackburn line in 1914. In the foreground is a special gun-powder train, complete with armed guard, possibly indicating its role as an ammunition train. All the vans are L&YR dia. 3 conversions, with the roof-doors filled in. Their cleanliness and immaculate paint-work suggests an ex-works condition. The vehicles are marked return empty to Gathurst *where a chemical/explosive works had long been established.*

B. C. LANE COLLECTION

bringing all railways and tramways under a single authority; (2) creation of a permanent body of railway managers to ensure the operation of the railways when they passed under state control; and (3) the creation of a consultative body which would bring together representatives of the railways and state departments to a mutual benefit.

At last everyone who mattered agreed, and the Railway Executive Committee was eventually formed at a meeting of the BoT on November 5th 1912. Its members were F. Ree (LNWR and acting chairman), H. A. Walker (LSWR and deputy chairman), J. A. F. Aspinall (L&YR), O. R. H. Bury (GNR), A. K. Butterworth (NER), Sir S. Fay (GCR), G. Garnett (MR), D. A. Matheson (CR), and F. Potter (GWR). In January 1913, Bury resigned and was replaced by the GNR's new general manager C. H. Dent. Five months later F. H. Dent of the South Eastern & Chatham was appointed as a representative of the BoT. This committee

served through the last few years of peace, and performed vital functions during the mobilisation exercises of 1913. It was greatly aided in this period by the Communications Board set up under clause 3 of Ree's recommendations, the members of that committee being of such standing in military and political fields that they could almost instantly give approval to any request from the Railway Executive. Interestingly the head of the Board was the Quarter-master General, Sir John Steven Cowans KCB, MVO. Though a military man through and through, he was eminently suited for the position, as he had a great personal interest

in railways and their operation. His father being the noted railway engineer John Cowans, who had worked for George Stephenson before starting his own firm of Cowans, Sheldon & Co. in 1846. So in a state of almost absolute preparation, the railways were ready for the events of August 1914.

Every soldier's nightmare – a Regimental Sergeant Major awaits the new arrivals at Winchester Station in August 1914. The scouts waiting with him were in fact used as messengers, and were not (as might be imagined) under-age recruits!

HAMPSHIRE RECORD OFFICE

State control begins

In reality, the British Government declared war on Germany at 11 pm (London time) on August 4th, which was midnight on the continent. Exactly one hour later the Railway Executive Committee took control of the railways, from its central office in the LNWR buildings at 35, Parliament St. Westminster. Just days before the declaration of war, a private telephone system had been completed, linking the committee's office to those of its regional control centres. These were at the offices of the L&YR in Manchester, the Midland at Derby, and the NER at York. Further links were installed between Parliament St., and the various Government and Military departments. Notice was sent to the railway companies, first by telephone, then by telegram, and later confirmed in writing by an order from the War Office. Therefore as from 00.01 on August 5th, two-thirds of Britain's railway companies came under state control.

Yet, the statement control is misleading for, in the main, it was anything but. The management structures, the administration, and to a large extent the traffic patterns remained, just as they had been in peacetime. What changed were the working arrangements, at least as far as important military and governmental traffic was concerned. Priorities being assigned to this, and imposed in addition to the mobilisation timetables agreed on beforehand by the respective companies. In this regard, some of the mobilisation programmes did seriously affect the normal operations of the individual companies, and in many cases lead to the curtailment and even the cancellation of several services. In some instances, particularly the London connecting lines and those leading to the cross-channel ports, the

Herbert A. Walker, General Manager of the London & South Western Railway, and chairman of the Railway Executive from May 1914 to December 1919. In fact both Ree and Walker were only acting-chairman, for officially the title chairman was vested in the President of the Board of Trade to provide an impartial head to whom inter-company disputes might be referred. Otherwise the acting-chairman held the real authority, and Walker used his to good effect right through the war years.

NATIONAL RAILWAY MUSEUM

As part of the mobilisation large quantities of railway equipment were released for military use on the order of the Railway Executive. On September 12th 1914, a train of 15 L&YR delivery drays is assembled and awaits departure from Newton Heath, Manchester, for Southampton, from where they will be shipped to France. NATIONAL RAILWAY MUSEUM

cuts were quite savage. However elsewhere, despite some delays, it was mostly business as usual.

In all, 130 companies were 'taken over', though 46 were not. Quite how the selection was made is uncertain, but obviously reference was made to those lines which had important strategic or economic importance. In such cases, the size of the undertaking was immaterial, as was the case with the small lines which provided useful connections between the major railways. Yet there were several anomalies. Many dock railway systems were taken over, but others like those at Felixstowe, the Manchester Ship Canal and Milford Haven were not. It was the same with the light mineral railways: for example, why exclude the Talyllyn, when the Festiniog was taken under the Executive's control?

Another apparent anomaly, the Killin Railway from Loch Tay, is more easily understood, when one considers the vital timber traffic which originated on it. Even so, it is inconceivable to think that the little Easingwold Railway, with just one tank loco, four coaches and ten trucks, could have had any possible military value to the state. By contrast, the Government grants provided to construct the Wick & Lybster (£25,000) and the Dornoch (£14,945) railways, now became apparent with the War Office revealing that they had supported construction of these lines. Though they were ostensibly constructed to serve local fishing communities, we may ask, had they actually been seen as the most expedient way of protecting those parts of the Scottish Coast? The Admiralty had long known of a theoretical plan to invade the remote coast, somewhere between Dornoch Point and Sinclairs Bay in order to cut supply routes to the important naval anchorages in northern Scotland. The construction of these lines reduced that threat, cutting down the isolated area to an acceptable 19 mile section between Helmsdale and Lybster.

It will be recalled that one of the objectives set by the War Railway Council, was to provide for and establish, new lines, connections, sidings and the like. Some of these will be discussed later, but four major works were immediately ordered by the Executive. All of these provided physical connections between other railways, and all were installed for strategic military reasons, primarily related to defence matters. The first was the double junction at Gospel Oak, joining the Tottenham & Hampstead Junction Railway and the LNWR; providing a through route between the LNWR and the GER and the London Tilbury and Southend section of the Midland Railway. Second, was another line off the T&HJR, allowing for a single track connection from near Crouch Station, to the GNR at Harringay. Next came a 'defensive link' between the Midland and GNR lines at Peterborough, but after little or no use, it was removed after the war. Finally, a 700 yd long link was provided between Whetstone on the GCR main line, and Blaby on the LNWR's South Leicester line.

Thus it came to be, that but for a few exceptions, all the railways of Britain could be regarded as a single system at the outbreak of war; inasmuch as they allowed the through passage of trains anywhere between Thurso and Penzance, or Margate and the Kyle of Localsh, all the separate and individual companies were working towards a common objective!

By contrast a number of lines carrying vital traffic were not taken into control, as for example, the Ravenglass Railway on the Cumberland coast. This line carried a considerable amount of iron-ore traffic in the pre-war years, most of which was consigned to steel works along the coast. It would almost certainly have been taken over as a controlled line, but for the fact that it had been closed since the depression of 1908. It re-opened after war was declared and despite its diminutive gauge, it continued to provide a vital link between the mines and quarries of Eskdale and the Furness Railway's coastal line between Barrow and Whitehaven.
RAVENGLASS & ESKDALE RAILWAY CO.

When the list of state controlled railways was drawn up, there were a few unusual inclusions amongst which was the little Easingwold Railway. From its junction with NER main line at Alne the little branch ambled into a rural back-water. Unless one considers the agricultural produce shipped along the branch, it is hard to imagine what strategic value the line could hold for the Executive Committee. After the war it was returned to private ownership, but what effect state control had on the company is difficult to say. In this post-war view, the company's solitary locomotive is seen at Easingwold with an ex-NER 6-wheeled coach.
T. J. EDGINGTON COLLECTION

The Mobilisation

So far as the mobilisation went, the Admiralty held a test run for its reserve forces on July 12-14th as the likelihood of war drew ever closer. In this regard several ships put to sea, and the demobilisation of these Naval Reservists was not fully completed before war was declared. Elsewhere, the Army Reservists, Militia, and the Territorials were called up on July 26th for the first of the annual training camps. The second series of camps were to commence on Sunday August 3rd, a problem which was compounded, by the fact that the Navy had decided to call up all its remaining reservists on the 2nd which fact alone required the running of 239 special trains. However, the railway companies foresaw immense difficulties with this, as civilian traffic would also peak on August 2nd because of the annual holidays. Feeling they would be unable to manage if war was declared that weekend, the Railway Executive asked the War Office to defer the second series of training camps, but surprisingly the Secretary of State refused.

It was a situation which had been unforseen in all the peace-time planning, and one which threatened to throw the whole mobilisation programme into chaos. By the Sunday morning, conditions on the continent were so grave, that many units arriving at stations to go away to camp, were turned back to their 'drill halls' on an order from the Secretary of State for War. Those en-route were often halted in mid-journey, and their trains turned back, others found that no sooner had they arrived at their camp, than they were sent home again. In addition to this, the recall of those who had been at camp since July 26th, imposed an immense strain on the railways that Sunday. For example, the little Cambrian Railway had to suddenly find 27 trains to transport 9,000 men from the Welsh Territorial camps at Aberystwyth and Portmadoc on what was their busiest weekend of the year. Down in the south, the tiny station at Amesbury on the L&SWR handled no less than 38 trains, sent to convey the forces of the Home Counties Brigade back home.

The general mobilisation came into effect from 00.01 on August 5th, coinciding with the state control of the railways. The programme of Mobilisation Days began at the same time, August 5th being day one. To avoid congestion at stations, each unit had an assembly day and time, therefore those with the order MOB+02-11 reported to their allotted railway stations at 11 am on the second day (ie the 6th) and so on. The mobilisation lasted for 14 days and took no special account of August 10th and 17th which were Sundays, but treated as normal working days. Each group was given a priority order in the mobilisation scheme, 1st) Territorials, 2nd) the Reservists, 3rd)

Two views of 'Calling men to the colours' in Dewsbury; the first is taken outside the Town Hall, with troops assembled in the square adjacent to the L&YR station. The curiously worded slogan on the buildings refers to the enlistment target set by the Town Council, which promised 2,000 men for the army. When this photograph was taken on August 19th 1914, the number of recruits had apparently reached one quarter of the target.

After parading in the town, the men were marched to one of Dewsbury's three passenger stations. They are seen here waiting to depart from the elevated island platform of Dewsbury GNR, many will be wearing uniforms made from woolen cloth produced in the town. Indeed, some may even be among the 1,287 textile workers who were later recalled from the army to work in the industry. The vast majority never returned, for these 'Pals' battalions suffered some of the heaviest casualties of the war.

BOTH KIRKLEES MUSEUMS & LIBRARIES

*It was not only men who were conscripted into
the armed forces, but as will be seen, the
fourth part of the Mobilisation Order was the
call up of horses for the Regular Army. In this
the railways played an important role, and
around 12% of its horses were released for this
purpose. On December 12th 1914 a train of
L&YR and LNWR cattle trucks are loaded at
a Lancashire station with horses which have
been requisitioned.*
NATIONAL RAILWAY MUSEUM

Special Reservists (the militia), 4th) Horses
for the regular army. During the mobilisation
period the number of trains run was
staggering, over 632 originated on the GWR
alone, whilst the LNWR supplied 550.

Initially, it has been planned for priority in
all cases to be given to the six infantry and
one cavalry divisions which had been formed
to make the British Expeditionary Force.
Pre-war plans had envisaged the
embarkation of this Force on the same day
as war was declared, but for various reasons
this did not begin until August 9th. This was
partly due to the concurrent demands placed
on the Railway Executive by different
Government departments, and the amended
orders for extra trains to be supplied to the
different Area Commands.

Therefore it was essential to re-model the
mobilisation timetables, and the BEF
embarkation was amended to commence
MOB+5. This did not greatly disrupt events,
and thanks to the smoothness of pre-war
planning, the required changes were easily
made. The first BEF train arrived at
Southampton at 8.48 am August 9th, with the
last arriving there at 6 pm on August 17th.
Altogether 334 trains ran, carrying the initial
force of 68,847 officers and men, 21,523
horses, 166 field guns, 2,446 vehicles, 1,368
bicycles, and 2,550 tons of stores. When the
reinforcement programme had been
completed by August 31st, some 670 trains

*An immediate priority for the Railway
Executive was the movement of the Regular
Army from its far-flung depots and barracks
around the British Isles. This was even more
difficult when many of these units were at
camp with the Territorial forces at the time,
as for example the Durham Light Infantry
who were on exercises in Weardale. On
August 5th, men assemble at Wolsingham
Station (NER) for the train which will take
them back to the RHQ in Durham.*
NORTH OF ENGLAND OPEN AIR MUSEUM, BEAMISH

had run in total, with commensurate
increases in the figures quoted above.

Again the information concerning the
mobilisation and the despatch of troops to
France is so great, it is impossible to recount
it all. Suffice it to say, the railway played a
supremely important role, as testified to by
the comments of Secretary of War,. Lord
Kitchener, in an address to the House of
Lords on August 25th:-

'The railway companies, in the all-
important matter of transport facilities, have
more than justified the complete confidence
reposed in them by the War Office, all
grades of railway services having laboured
with untiring energy and patience.'

Troop Trains

Great as the mobilisation was, it might be regarded as just the tip of the iceberg. Whereas the numbers of troops carried in the initial period could be counted in tens of thousands, those which followed were numbered in millions. Additionally, whilst those moved under the mobilisation followed a pre-ordained plan, the later troop traffic was subject to different arrangements. Apart from a short period at the end of 1914, all subsequent troop movements were coordinated by the Army Area Commands which we discussed in the introduction.

It will be recalled that to each Command was appointed a secretary railway company, through which all railway matters were handled. This system remained basically un-altered throughout the war, although in 1915 the South Eastern & Chatham company was superseded by the LNWR as the secretary company for the Eastern Command. This was due to the heavy administrative duties already engaged in by the SE&CR, who were inundated with work pertaining to the lines supplying the channel-ports. On the other hand, the much larger LNWR were able to absorb the work in spite of already acting as secretary company to the Western Area Command.

The work of these secretary companies was most interesting, and largely involved the complete reversal of normal railway administrative practice: ie, the working of train routes and timetables from the destination backwards! Though quite confusing, it was an essential requirement for the War Office, who had to have troops at certain embarkation ports at a specified time in order for them and their baggage to be loaded onto the correct ships. Therefore an Area Command would be issued with the War Office directive that A, B and C battalions of X regiment, embark Folkestone at such and such a time. This command would be addressed to the secretary company, along with a note of what was to be carried. Firstly the company would plan what stock was needed, ie: the number of first-class coaches for officers, the seating accommodation for NCOs and enlisted men, cattle trucks for horses, box vans for stores, and open wagons of artillery, vehicles etc.It would then ascertain if the train could be worked through to its destination by a single locomotive and crew, or if it would have to be handed on to another company en-route.

If the train was to be worked through to its destination as a single unit, a number of important issues had first to be resolved. Most importantly, could the stock of the originating company comply with the loading gauge of the receiving railway, and any others it might pass through on its journey? Likewise, would the locomotives assigned to the task be within any axle-loading restrictions on the lines on which it would travel? Both of these points were especially critical in East Anglia, Northern Scotland and certain parts of Wales. Further, it was essential that pilot drivers were available when a through train reached the junction with another company, for it was impractical to send men along lines of which they could not possibly have any route knowledge. Arrangements would have to be made in

---

The 3rd Royal Fusiliers await their troop train at Hook Station on August 20th 1914. They are pictured with the boy scouts who had acted as runners for the soldiers whilst they were camped in Hampshire, until the regiment was shipped out to France. Note the lady seated centre, and the railway staff looking on.
HAMPSHIRE RECORD OFFICE

respect of watering and coaling the locomotive, in addition to food or lodging for the train crew if they were away from their home shed over a specified length of time. Finally, it had to be seen if there could be any counter-balancing traffic, which would obviate the wasteful, empty return workings. Such considerations all weighed heavily against the system of through trains, but a great many were run for expediency's sake. Indeed as the war progressed, many drivers became so adept at taking their charges over 'foreign' systems, they were able to do this without pilots.

Generally speaking, the vast majority of crews handed over trains at the inter-company boundaries, where locomotives of that system would take over. Whilst this reduced the number of 'foreign' locos seen on some lines, the same could not be said of coaching and goods stock. For example, one photograph submitted for this book (though not used because of its poor quality) showed Highland Railway passenger stock at Avonmouth Docks. Another view presented GCR coaches in Inverness. Obviously the secretary companies still had to be mindful of the various loading gauge restrictions and the need for counter-balancing but, by careful routing, most trains were able to work all the way to their destination. This minimised the waste of time involved in

Arriving at Folkestone, Soldiers from an un-identified regiment arrive at the port in 1917. The picture presents a fascinating view of the docks and railways during a period when access to the area was actively restricted. Note the dredger which was kept in continuous employment to allow deep-draughted vessels access to the wharves.
NATIONAL RAILWAY MUSEUM

many men in this duty as did its mighty neighbour the GWR. Each company worked its 'military' department in the way best suited to its own peculiar needs and according to how it interpreted the Railway Executive's orders, but most followed a fairly standard pattern. Therefore, men in the Great North of Scotland Railway, could easily communicate with their counterparts at the Cheshire Lines Committee and so on.

These Military Staffs did immensely valuable liaison work between the railway and the army, and were often called upon to sort out some very awkward situations. They were, so to speak, at the sharp end of the stick, a stick prodded with considerable ferocity by certain military commanders intent on having their own wishes complied with. This largely came from a general misconception of the meaning 'state control of railways' by many officers who believed the railway companies were under martial law. Therefore, local commanders often held the view that railways in *their* district were under *their* command. It therefore irked

Later on the same day, Princess Henrietta *is embarking troops before departing from Folkestone. The numbers of men boarding the paddle steamer is so large, that a definite list has developed to starboard. To the left of the picture the troop trains which brought the men to the port can be clearly seen.*
NATIONAL RAILWAY MUSEUM

threw an immense burden on the small staff employed in each secretary section; though in reality they were assisted by the Military Railway Staff in each of the companies they worked with. The staff of these military sections was usually around 15 in number; regardless of the size of the particular concern, the maximum rarely exceeded 22. For example the tiny Taff Vale employed as

detraining and entraining the troops each time they reached the boundary of one system. In this respect, the back-timing of troop trains was even more important than in those instances where they were worked to their destination by a single engine. For example, a train from Glasgow to Southampton might be worked by the CR, then change at Carlisle to the Midland, at Mexborough it would be handed over to the GCR who would take it as far as the GWR at Banbury, from there it would be taken to Basingstoke and the L&SWR. If the train had to be at Southampton by 5 pm, the programme of hand-over times would be worked back, with a fifteen minute buffer on each time to allow for contingencies. Eventually the Caledonian would be given a time at which the Midland would take the train, and after subtracting its journey time, the time for departure from Glasgow would be arrived at.

At first glance, this system apparently

Equipment train at Newton Heath, with 10 army water carts behind L&YR 0-6-0, No. 288. These water carts were part of an order for 35 such vehicles, each with a 118 gallons capacity galvanised tank. Pumping and filtering apparatus was included, and the water was discharged through a series of taps placed on a cross pipe at the end of the cart. The six-wheeled 'Tin-Tab' brake-van is from Wigan shed.

NATIONAL RAILWAY MUSEUM

them considerably, when some upstart had the afrontery to tell them they couldn't have the trains they wanted. In several instances it is reported that local station-masters were put under armed guard for failing to 'do as they were ordered'. It was a difficult situation, and one which called for immense tact. However, the Military Railway Staff had to firmly point out, they were under direct orders from the War Office, and that if General so-and-so wanted a special train to take him and his wife to London, then the General would have to clear it with the Army Area Command. After the first few months of war these problems gradually died down, and from the end of 1915 onwards only the most cordial of relations are recorded.

It was also the duty of these small 'staffs' to prepare, type up, and duplicate all the timetables pertaining to troop movements that originated in their company's area. These documents were often quite extensive and, because of the nature of the trains, highly confidential. Therefore, even the most routine matters dealt with by these departments had to be handled solely by the small number of men employed in them. For example, right from the outbreak of war, it was practice to fix a sticky label in the windows on the front and rear coaches of troop trains. These labels, even though they bore nothing more than the class and number of the train, were classified as secret. It was the duty of the Military Railway Staff to see the labels were affixed to the train windows, and any surplus ones were immediately burnt. As a matter of interest, these labels were printed in red, and had a single letter, below which was printed three digits. The letter signified the class of train, the digits its number on the general orders, therefore X 123 would be British Expeditionary Force, train No. 123.

Finally, it might be mentioned that the workers employed in connection with these military duties enjoyed a considerable degree of power. For, instance they could comandeer motor vehicles, omnibuses and taxis; they could take over trains on behalf of the executive; and even turf out passengers, travelling on other trains to make way for important journeys by military or naval personnel. Their offices were never closed, being open 24 hours a day, seven days a week. The department's telephones were always continually manned (usually by an operator loaned from the General Post Office), and a motorbike was available for urgent despatches. Thereby, the railway companies were always accessible for any orders which they might be given by the Area Commands concerning troop movements, or any other instructions which might be sent from either the secretary company, or the Railway Executive.

The strangest of all troop trains, a wind-powered inspection cart on the Spurn Point Military Railway. The line itself was built in connection with the Humber Estuary Defence Scheme, and manned by the Royal Engineers. Few photographs of this railway have survived, and this view presents a rare example on a rare line – if any reader has other photographs, both the author and the Hull museums would dearly like to hear about them.

CITY OF KINGSTON UPON HULL, MUSEUMS & ART GALLERIES

Civilian Traffic & Travel Restrictions

Initially, both the press and the railway companies presented the facade that, but for some minor inconveniences, it was to be business as usual. Indeed, had not the war been so prolonged, along with the demand for the release of men and locomotives for service in France, then it may well have been possible to keep up this pretence. During the 14 days of the mobilisation, there were (as might be expected) numerous delays and cancellations to services. This coincided with the main holiday period of 1914, but even so the general public were not overly inconvenienced by it all. The suspension of cheap travel and certain excursion tickets was lifted as early as August 22nd, and many who had been prevented from holidaying earlier that month took the opportunity to travel on the last weekend of August. For example the Down Cornish Riviera ran in no less than 18 parts that Saturday. In fact, if anything, civilian traffic increased throughout the autumn, and this without taking into account people who were using the trains in connection with matters related to the war: ie, Munitions Workers, troops on leave, etc.

By the start of 1915, the reduction in manpower due to the numbers flocking to 'the colours' was beginning to affect the railway companies, but few realised that they were witnessing the greatest war in history unfold. Those at home now found themselves with more and more money to spend, largely due to the increased output in the manufacturing industries. Record wages, and in many cases reduced hours, allowed certain sections of the community more freedom to travel. Joy-riding increased, but along with it, so did the numbers of troop trains, coal trains, and military traffic, a problem compounded by the transfer of virtually all the East Coast shipping traffic on to the railways. The worsening situation was referred to the C14 committee of the Railway Executive, made up from 24 Superintendents of the Line. In meetings held at the Lancashire & Yorkshire Rly's offices in Great College Street, Westminster, various proposals were made for restricting passenger travel, and where possible discouraging it – especially joy-riding. First

King George V and Queen Mary arrive at Dewsbury LNWR station to inspect the various textile mills and clothing factories in the Heavy Woollen District which were involved in uniform manufacturing. Mill workers were given a days holiday, all except those in the factories where the Royal couple were to visit.
KIRKLEES MUSEUMS & LIBRARIES

of these resulted in the withdrawal of 180 competitive trains, all of which duplicated services on other routes. This was followed by the suspension of cheap tickets etc, though once again there were many groups and classes who could still claim travel at reduced rates. These schemes had no appreciable affect, and so, on the Monday before Easter, the availability of the remaining cheap-travel classes was further reduced. Easter came and went, and with it an overall increase of 30% in passenger traffic. In summer the increase was even greater, and almost equalled the record summer of 1913.

The hard-pressed South Eastern & Chatham was faced with an impossible situation, which it addressed later in 1915 by closing several halts and small stations – a move followed by the Midland, Highland and Great Northern railways. The GER tried to follow suit and announced the proposed closure of no fewer than nineteen stations;

the uproar which followed succeeded in reducing the number to fourteen. A further method was seen to increase the capacity of trains, and although an unpalatable measure, January 1916 saw the wide scale withdrawal of restaurant and sleeping car services on many lines in the south. In April the LNWR followed suit on the west coast route, and to prevent them gaining an unfair advantage, this was matched by those companies on the East Coast lines. In May, tourist tickets were suspended, ostensibly for the summer, but in September the order was confirmed for the duration of the war. Notwithstanding all these various reductions in cheap fares, numbers of trains, lack of buffet facilities etc, traffic receipts were considerably higher that Easter. So, to discourage any similar occurrence at Whitsuntide, a Royal Proclamation was made postponing the bank holiday until August 8th, when it would be added to the August Bank Holiday. Traffic on the railways was even greater, as many who had previously booked Whitsun holidays were unable or unwilling to cancel them. The Government, now fearful of the demands on the railways that summer, decided to cancel the August holidays indefinitely, and asked people to stay at home – fat chance! In two days alone, the L&YR handled over 1,000 trains at its stations in Blackpool and Fleetwood, whilst the LB&SCR ran its principal Brighton express in 21 parts. It

seemed, no matter what restrictions were imposed, the public had worked hard for the war effort and earned a holiday which they were jolly well going to have!

This was concurrent with the increasing strain imposed by military traffic on the railways, and the demands of the War Office and Ministry of Munitions for yet more men and locomotives to be released for service in France. The Ministry said it would accept no less than 370 freight engines by the end of the year, a quantity which it was impossible to release with the high level of traffic on the railways at home. At the same time, the Ministry of Munitions compounded the problem, by making it even more difficult for the companies to get the vital raw materials needed by the railway workshops to repair 'failed' locomotives. In September, the Executive announced the number of locomotives awaiting repairs or major overhaul was no less than 476. If 'the powers that be' had been possessed with any sense, they would have seen the solution to both the overseas and home problems sitting on rusted sidings around

the various workshops and engine sheds. True, the types of these 'dead' locos were not what may have been needed for France, but by various juggling acts the railways could almost have instantly supplied what was required. However, it was not to be, and the repair and renewal programme was badly hampered by this fact.

Faced with this stone-wall approach, the Railway Executive had no option but to ask its C14 Superintendent's Committee to look at further ways of achieving travel restrictions which would allow the release of men and machines for France. It came out heavily against the introduction of travel permits, and instead proposed a system of cuts and restrictions that makes

Dr. Beeching look like Santa Claus. How a group of such dedicated railway operators could make these decisions is today beyond comprehension, for in hindsight so many of these 'cuts' left the railways with a legacy from which some lines never recovered. Take for example the little Brampton Town branch of the NER in Cumberland; it was closed on the order of the Executive, despite the fact that over 500 workers were daily using it to travel to the munition works at Gretna and Longtown. The branch re-opened after the war, but like so many others, its patronage had been forced on to bus or tram services, and within a few years it was closed once again – permanently.

It was not only stations and branches

As early as February 1915, the Railway Executive Committee recognised that a shortage of good quality steam coal would ensue if the war became a protracted affair. In March the committee ordered the railway companies to lay in reserve stocks, and by April coal orders from the 12 larger companies had increased by 25%. Coal stacked for emergency use at the GER's Stratford depot, is seen arrayed in superbly built stacks, the art of which owes much to dry-stone walling techniques.
NATIONAL RAILWAY MUSEUM

which were closed, but whole lines of track were ripped up and shipped off to France: sacrificed to the all-important *god* of munitions for the front. In addition to such closures, fares were increased by a hefty 50% and nearly all forms of concessionary travel were abolished in an attempt to discourage public use of the trains. Yet, who at the same time was giving concessionary tickets to its workers, encouraging them to travel home, to the seaside, or just to visit friends? Yes, none other than the Ministry of Munitions!

In order to accomplish these savage cuts, the Board of Trade had to seek powers under the Defence of the Realm Act in order to avoid the legal, technical and contractual obligations which it would have been faced with under pending legislation. There was an understandable up-roar, and Questions were asked in parliament to which the Minister of Munitions replied:-

' The Government is satisfied it can look confidently to the public cheerfully to put up with the restrictions.'

The public didn't, but there was less cheering news to follow. Personal luggage, and luggage sent in advance was limited to a maximum weight of 100 lbs (250 lbs for an officer in uniform). Express trains were decelerated and made to stop at intermediate stations, and many stopping trains were reduced. Mixed trains, that is to say made up of passenger and freight stock, were to be introduced, despite the fact that this practice had long been condemned by the Accident Inspectors of the BoT. The number of closed stations was increased to over 400, whilst the majority of those remaining open were closed from 10 pm on Saturday to 6 am on a Monday. Almost all the remaining cheap fare concessions were removed, with only a few noted examples like ship-wrecked mariners, poor children/orphans and volunteer nurses left un-touched. Season ticket holders were also faced with some severe increases and restrictions, particularly when it was found that there was growing abuse of the system. One such abuse was from continental refugees who had set up thriving businesses in London. Fearful of the bombing raids on the city, they took to purchasing season tickets for stations on the Brighton and Thames Valley lines in order to escape for the night when an attack was on. One working to Maidenhead was so badly abused by these 'season ticket holders', railwaymen dubbed it the "Palestine Express".

By the spring of 1918 these cuts had finally appeared to have succeeded in reducing public rail travel, but when Easter came round again, the demand for tickets exceeded that for 1913 by 22%. More cuts followed, but this only saw an overall reduction of around 7% in non-military/munitions related passenger miles, indicating the British public's insatiable and un-ending desire for rail travel, despite all the means initiated to prevent if from so doing!

However, this extra coaling work presented an awkward situation, as there were insufficient men to handle all the extra work this entailed due to the enlistment of large numbers of railway staff in the forces. To meet this short-fall in staff, troops under training or prisoners of war were often drafted in to work on the railway, as can be seen at Newton Heath where coaling is being undertaken.
NATIONAL RAILWAY MUSEUM

Naval Traffic

It has been seen how well the military had prepared for the coming conflict, and all the advanced planning evolved through the Army Railway Council. Regretfully, it was not the same situation with the Admiralty, who's transport arrangements were found to be quite inadequate in the summer of 1914. It was not that the Navy did not have the required facilities, they did; however, they were mostly in the wrong places. For centuries, naval development had been geared to dealing with threats from our 'natural enemies', France and Spain, and therefore the bulk of the Admiralty's dockyards, ports and stores were situated on the southern coast between Chatham in the east, and Dartmouth in the west. As these establishments were not ideally located to deal with the new threat from across the North Sea, facilities had to be provided on the north east coasts of England and Scotland, a situation met by moving the Grand Fleet to an anchorage at Scapa Flow, between Scotland and the Orkneys, from where it would be more able to deal with the German Navy.

Those familiar with the geography of this remote region, will immediately realise what problems this presented for transporting men and essential supplies. Prior to 1914, supplies for naval craft away from the main dockyards was done by Fleet Auxiliary ships. However, supplying the Scottish anchorages by sea was inviting the attention of enemy submarines and commerce raiders, so most of this traffic was sent by rail to stations at Aberdeen, Grangemouth, Invergordon and Thurso. Traffic concerned with the fleet can roughly be divided into four groups 1) naval personnel, 2) supplies of coal and fuel oil, 3) ordnance, and 4) victuals and provisions. So complex was the movement of traffic between the main naval establishments and operational bases, it is only possible to present a brief summary in this book.

At the outbreak of the war the Navy had no facilities for sending coal by rail, yet by the end of 1919 it had secured the use of over 16,000 wagons. The bulk of these were used to carry steam coal from South Wales. Three railways, the GWR, the Rhymney, and the Taff Vale, gathered the traffic and took it to Pontypool Road (GWR), where it was

marshalled into trains and forwarded to the LNWR at Warrington. At Carlisle it passed on to the Caledonian who conveyed it to Perth; there a Rail Transport Officer allocated it to the various bases to which it was forwarded by the Caledonian, Highland and Great North of Scotland railways. In later years, additional routes were used, involving the L&YR, NBR, NER and Midland companies to increase the carrying capacity. By May 1919, it was recorded that almost $5\frac{1}{2}$ million tons of coal had passed north of Pontypool Road, and this figure does not include that sent to English ports.

Supplies for Navy vessels were always

The Jellicoe Specials, so named after the Admiral of the Grand Fleet, can be divided into two types; those which carried coal for the fleet, and the special Euston-Thurso express trains which ran to convey officers and rating to their ships at the new naval bases in the far north. Inverness became almost a closed station, and there were numerous alterations to the station layout, with several timber-built platform extensions being erected. In the spring of 1918 a 'Jellicoe Express' arrives at the town, made up from a variety of mixed stock supplied by different companies. Of interest are the special ticket or pass barriers erected from sheep hurdles.
ROYAL NAVAL MUSEUM, PORTSMOUTH

wanted on a priority, with arrival times having to coincide with the all too short a period when a ship might be in port. Therefore goods traffic consigned for naval establishments was often sent by passenger train to ensure its arrival within the specified period. Even bulky items like propellors were sent thus, located on special wagons suitably marshalled in the passenger train. In the south traffic might be moved more leisurely to the main Naval dockyards, but in the far north their was no warehousing available for storage. A few existing warehouses were taken over to alleviate this problem, but even so, it became the norm to run special trains to provision individual ships and squadrons directly. In Scotland, this involved a whole variety of special arrangements, including the provision of many extra sidings and passing loops. At Inverness a new branch line was required to link the station with quay, it was laid and open within two weeks, despite having to demolish several houses to provide the needed access. In other places whole lines were swallowed up, as was the case with the Highland Railway's branches to Keith and Buckie, both of which were taken up to provide track for the U.S. Navy mine depot at Dalmore near Invergordon.

Following on from the adoption of the Scottish anchorages, it remained for the

Navy to arrange transport for men serving on the ships stationed there. The movement of naval personnel was, by the nature of ship movements described above, very irregular. As it was not possible to provide all the men joining or leaving their ships with accommodation on scheduled passenger trains, a naval special was run each weekday from Euston at 6 pm as from February 15th 1915, timed to arrive in Thurso at 3.30 pm the next day and involving a journey of 717 miles. At Crewe the train was joined by through coaches from Plymouth, the passengers on which would have an 834 mile journey. Connecting services were run from Milford Haven, Cardiff, Birkenhead, Liverpool, Southampton, Portsmouth, Brighton, Chatham, Dover, Tilbury, Harwich, Hull, Newcastle, Stranraer, and Barrow-in-Furness. This naval passenger system might have placed an additional burden on Britain's railways, but by it there was a regular movement between the major naval ports in England, Scotland and Wales, a system whereby naval officers and ratings, and even essential stores or supplies could be despatched to any ship or shore establishment on the mainland within 24 hours.

Tank Traffic

By the autumn of 1914, the battle-lines in France were drawn up for a war of attrition. The open battle-fields of previous centuries were replaced, and in their stead there sprang up rows of trenches. This new type of war presented a terrifying face, where countless lives were offered in a ritual sacrifice as infantry and cavalry attacks were no answer to the supremacy of machine guns. From one offensive to the next, the war continued thus for over two years. On July 1st 1916 the Battle of the Somme began, but the stalemate remained. On that first day over 60,000 British casualties were recorded, but by September neither side had made any appreciable gain and the offensive appeared to have lost its impetus. Then around 6 am on the morning of the 15th, the strongly entrenched Germans beheld block-like shapes moving ponderously out of the mists towards them. Thus began the Battle of Flers-Courcelette, where tank warfare was first employed.

Tanks had been developed by the

Landships Committee, envisaged as a means for making substantial in-roads into enemy territory; using armour-plated, tracked vehicles for penetrating the forests of barbed wire and crossing vast seas of mud, impervious to withering machine-gun fire. Most British tanks came from the Metropolitan Carriage Wagon & Finance Co's works in Birmingham, but others were built by Armstrong Whitworth in Newcastle, Brown Brothers in Edinburgh, Coventry

Trainload of tanks leaving Lincoln (the Cathedral is just visible in the background of the original print), probably Mark I tanks in the very first months of tank warfare. Note that all the vehicles are sheeted over in an attempt to disguise the tanks, the rail vehicles on which they are mounted are standard types and not specially designed for the considerable weights they were asked to carry. THE TANK MUSEUM

Ordnance Works in Glasgow, Fosters of Lincoln, Kitson & Co. in Leeds, and The North British Loco Co. in Glasgow. Each of these factories had a testing ground, and when a tank had been accepted for service it would be consigned to Avonmouth Docks or the training camp at Bovington in Dorset. As these destinations were all a considerable distance from the manufacturing plants, the slow moving tanks could not cover the distance under their own power. As there were no suitable road-transporters, the railway system was the only way of moving them, though so secret was this traffic, every tank was securely sheeted down.

The earliest tanks (Mark I and two small batches of training tanks) were well outside the loading gauge, and therefore had to have their sponsons bodily removed before they could be shipped by rail. The first tank

Mark IV (female) tank, 'Auld Reekie II' of A Battalion Tank Corps. Weight 28 tons plus trench crossing fascine, bending a bolster wagon at Plateau railhead France, November 1917, before Cambrai. The transportation of tanks continued to present a problem throughout the war years for even after the development of the Rectank wagons there were never sufficient numbers of these special vehicles to entirely eliminate the use of standard rail wagons. THE TANK MUSEUM

A Mark I tank, with sponsons removed to conform with the loading gauge, mounting a wagon in the works of William Foster & Co., Lincoln. The Russian inscription reading 'With Care to Petrograd' was a naive camouflage; notice the rear steering tail that characterised the early tanks. THE TANK MUSEUM

training ground was established at Thetford, Norfolk, on the estate of Lord Iveagh. To facilitate the secret movements, the GER laid a siding into the grounds and constructed a special dock-platform so that un-loading could be accomplished out of public view. As the traffic grew, the railway company provided a further siding for one of its withdrawn dining-car sets which was sent to cater for the staff there. Once the tanks had

undergone trials, they were loaded on special trains at Barnham and despatched to either Southampton or Avonmouth. By 1918, a central testing station was opened at Newbury and when the 'secret' port of Richborough opened, all tank traffic was sent that way.

As there were no special rail-transporters, at first all tanks were carried on standard rail wagons. Mostly these were of the bogie-bolster type, despite the fact that few were really happy with the 28 ton loads placed upon them. The NER and Caledonian had a few special vehicles associated with the steel and shipbuilding industries, which were more readily suited to tank-transport. However, these were too few in number and already had enough existing commitments

as not to make any appreciable difference. Elsewhere boiler wagons were tried with some effect, but again the designs were not sufficiently suitable to produce them in the required numbers. To overcome the problem, the Railway Executive ascertained the requirements of the military and commissioned the design and manufacture of special vehicles: a transporter code-named 'RECTANK' and an associated ramp-wagon, types of which then first entered service in 1917.

At least two accidents befell tank trains, the first of which was between Sway and Brockenhurst in the New Forest. A Birmingham-Wool (for Bovington) train was crossing an embankment when a tank broke loose and swung round on its wagon. This

Plateau railhead; tank trains forming up for distribution of tanks to Battalion railheads: Battle of Cambrai, November 1917. Motive power is provided by a variety of ROD locomotives but the Army's preference for six-coupled tender engines is clearly evident.
THE TANK MUSEUM

was then hit by a north-bound train, and along with four other wagons and their loads it plunged down the embankment. The second incident occurred at Bournemouth Central, when the driver of another Bovington-bound train misjudged his braking and over-ran the signals, colliding into the rear of a stationary train.

Tanks for Bovington were detrained at Wool and driven two miles along a road to the camp. Towards the end of the war, this very substantial traffic was creating problems which were referred to the Railway

As tank warfare developed, so did the tanks and the rail vehicles used to move them. In this view a Mark V tank is seen on a Rectank at Metropolitan Works, Birmingham. The Rectank wagons and the associated ramp wagons were specially designed by a sub-committee of the Railway Executive which was supplemented by two army officers who had assisted on the landships committee.
THE TANK MUSEUM

Executive. In the summer of 1918, a plan for an extension was approved with the L&SWR to supply the required track. The work was completed just after the armistice, and an 0-6-0 from the Weymouth Tramway was

allocated to provide motive power. Today, part of the camp forms the home for the historic collection of preserved armoured fighting vehicles which make up the Tank Museum.

Air Raids

For the man in the street, Britain was an Island Fortress, the great power of the Navy providing an immense defensive wall, against everything but hit and run attacks from the German Navy. The threat from bombing seemed even more remote, for the range and capability of German aircraft was such that they would barely be able to penetrate the south eastern counties. Yet, as early as 1912, informed observers had warned of the potential threat from the great airships of Count Ferdinand von Zeppelin. However, it was an aeroplane that made the first aerial attack every experienced on Britain's railways, on Christmas Day 1914, when the LT&SR line was bombed between Standford-le-Hope and Low Street stations. The first of the airship raids was made on January 19th 1915, when Kapitan-Leutnant Fritze in Zeppelin L3 attacked Norfolk and succeeded in creating considerable damage to the railways at Kings Lynn docks. To discuss all the raids of the following four years would not be prudent, for the vast majority were almost total failures; and the damage sustained was so light, repairs were normally *effected within a few hours.* So we will confine our attention to more serious raids, like that at Wallsend on April 14th, when a train just avoided derailment when the track was bombed in front of it.

The east coast was frequently attacked that spring, even though the objective was the total destruction of London by a Great Fire Raid. One raid on August 12th again progressed only to the coast, but bombs dumped on Parkeston Station badly injured a loco cleaner and a fireman. On September 7th London was badly mauled, and 23 bombs fell around Euston, Holborn and Liverpool St. stations. In October a raid against the L&SWR's important junction at Croydon was less successful, though the bombs killed

nine civilians living nearby. Another Zeppelin caused damage to Leeman Street Station, which had the misfortune to be quite badly damaged two nights later in a further raid. That was the last serious raid of the year, but on January 31st 1916 the attacks were resumed with a vengeance. In an extensive raid on the Midlands, severe damage was caused to railway installations at Wednesbury, Tipton and Burton. In Derby, the raiders specifically aimed their attention at the Midland Railway's headquarters, doing their best to destroy the works. Large sections of the plant were damaged, causing severe disruption to all departments. A similar raid was planned against Sheffield on March 5th, but prevailing head winds forced the airships to dump their bombs on Humberside. Damage was done to the GCR's electric tramway and steam lines at Immingham Halt, but it was just one of the 53 Zeppelin raids this district suffered.

On March 31st, attention was turned against the munition factories, particularly those at Stowmarket, Erith and Woolwich Arsenal. But once again the raiders had little success. Three weeks later, a bomb was dropped at Fairlop on the Chigwell line, wrecking the station master's house. The raids of September 2nd-3rd became known as 'Zepp Sunday' when no less than eighteen enemy airships left their bases to attack England. Despite the size of the attacking force little damage is recorded to railway property; the only serious problem was at Boston, where a GNR signalman was badly injured. That night the first Zeppelin was shot down, and this signalled the end of the great raids. Though in a sneak attack on September 23rd, the stations at Streatham Common and Streatham Hill were struck by 600lb bombs. More bombs were dropped at Nottingham, causing damage to both the GNR and GCR lines out of the city.

On June 13th 1917, three bombs landed on Liverpool Street Station during a daylight

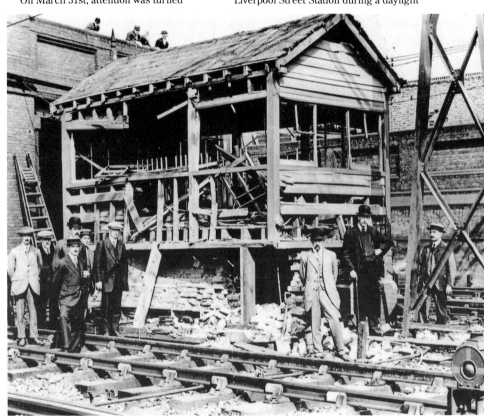

In ARP development, the railways played an important role, with several anti-aircraft weapons being designed and produced in railway workshops. This was not all, for at least two workshops were involved in the production of shells and tracer bullets designed to bring down the giant German airships. To illuminate the raiders as they passed over the cities, giant search-lights were produced in large numbers, a small batch of which were converted from naval types at the GNR's Doncaster plant.

NATIONAL RAILWAY MUSEUM

raid. The 12 noon train for Hunstanton standing at Platform 8 was badly damaged, and two coaches standing in the adjacent bay platform received a direct hit. These were in use as a medical centre for the recruiting service; as a result, sixteen men were killed and 23 injured. An equally nasty raid came on the night of September 29th/30th when a projectile crashed through the roof of the drivers' dormitory at Stratford, killing one driver outright and injuring two others. Three locomotives nearby were slightly damaged. On January 28th 1918, a train of empty carriages was hit as it left Cannon Street Station, considerably damaging one third class coach. But probably the worst attack of all was on March 17th, when five bombs fell in the vicinity of St. Pancras Station and the Midland Grand Hotel. One failed to explode, but the other four claimed 20 lives, mostly people sheltering under a covered carriage drive leading from the hotel to the main booking hall. The last of the German raids was August 5th 1918, when three airships approached Great Yarmouth. One was shot down and the two remaining craft turned and fled for home. In all, 24 railway workers were killed during bombing between December 1914 and August 1918.

The Humber ports of Grimsby, Hull and Immingham, and to a lesser extent Goole, were the frequent targets of German Zeppelins. Often Hull was as far as they could reach because of strong head-winds, and they would dump their bombs willy-nilly across any likely target they saw. However, and unlike the raids of World War 2, the attacks resulted in minimal damage. The strength of the explosives was very light, as can be seen by the crater left by a bomb which landed in between a series of timber sidings served by the Hull & Barnsley Railway.

CITY OF KINGSTON UPON HULL, MUSEUMS & ART GALLERIES

Accidents & disasters

As might be appreciated, the level of rail traffic grew considerably during World War One, a considerable proportion of which involved the transportation of highly dangerous consignments, including explosives and poisonous gasses. In addition, railway safety was prejudiced by a number of dangerous factors, including 1) increased troop and naval traffic, 2) transfer of coast-wise traffic from shipping to railways, 3) the enlistment of railwaymen in the armed forces and their replacement by less experienced staff, 4) the Ministry of Munitions' refusal to release much needed material for the maintenance of locos and stock, and 5) significantly lower standards of track maintenance and replacement. Those who have read our companion series, Trains In Trouble, will recognise all this as presenting the recipe for disaster. As many of the accidents between August 1914 and December 1918 have been discussed in that series, it is not intended to cover the same ground in these pages.

The year 1915 might be considered as the most horrific, for it was to see four exceptionally bad accidents. The scene was set on New Year's Day, when the driver of a Great Eastern express from Clacton to

Quintinshill was undoubtedly one of the most horrific accidents ever recorded in British railway history. The facts concerning the accident have been well documented in the Trains In Trouble series, but the role the war played in the events that fateful May morning are not so widely known. Firstly, all the trains involved were military specials or busier than normal because of the war. Added to this, the passing loops all down the Caley line were in continuous use due to the excessive number of additional trains using the route. Indeed, those loops were so continuously used, it is a wonder that the sloppy working practices at Quintinshill had not led to an accident before. Finally, despite the fact that a large number of men were gathered in the box when signalman Tinsley cleared his signals for the troop train, they were all too preoccupied discussing newspaper war reports to notice his mistake.
Upper picture: The twisted and mangled wreckage that was once a train.
Lower picture: The pitiful number of survivors from the troop train stand in a field alongside the line whilst an officer reads out the roll-call.
BOTH DUMFRIES & GALLOWAY LIBRARY SERVICE – DUMFRIES REFERENCE LIBRARY

London failed to stop at a distant signal. At the west end of Ilford station it struck a local train to Gidea Park in a violent side-long collision which claimed 10 lives and resulted in 500 injuries. On Easter Monday there was a spectacular run-away and crash at Burnham, on the Somerset & Dorset Joint. Yet this was nothing on the scale of what was to follow on May 15th, when a five-train crash occurred at a way-side passing loop north of Gretna. In the carnage at Quintinshill, over 227 lives were lost, with 224 more injured, a figure which has never been exceeded in any British railway disaster. On August 14th the spectre of inadequate maintenance reared its ugly head at Weedon, when the Irish Mail was derailed at high-speed. The simple loss of a pin and locking collar claiming no less than ten dead and 64 injured. In almost ghoulish glee, the mis-fortune which had dogged 1915 decided to have a final fling just two weeks before the end of the year at St. Bede's Junction on the North Eastern Railway. There a signalman's error, and a lack of diligence by the driver of a banking engine lead to a double collision which was attended by a fire; the disaster accounted for 18 lives and left 81 passengers with injuries and burns.

The year 1916 kicked off with something even more spectacular, though fortunately not very serious, when the Penistone Viaduct collapsed. On the viaduct at the time was an L&YR tank engine, which was precipitated to the bottom of the Don Valley. An urgent shortage of locomotives saw some remarkable attempts to recover the engine, but the steep sided valley and the atrocious weather prevented a successful outcome. After the comparative quiet of 1916, a major accident at Ratho on the North British Railway claimed twelve lives on January 3rd 1917. On September 15th a rake of ten six-wheeled NER coaches forming a troop train

When Penistone viaduct collapsed tank engine No. 661 was thrown to the bed of the valley. Despite the sheer drop, it was not badly damaged. In view of the very acute traffic situation a concerted effort was made to recover it from it lay. Regretfully all the attempts failed due to the steepness of the valley sides, and the atrocious weather conditions that February. Eventually the unfortunate engine was cut up on site and the remains were hauled away to Horwich works in wagons.
AUTHOR'S COLLECTION

ran away down the branch railway at Catterick Camp, derailing on a sharp curve and killing three soldiers. A fortnight later another NER engine came to grief near Hawes Junction, when the locomotive's leading axle snapped. January 1918 saw another bad start to the year, as seven fatalities are recorded at Little Salkeld, where a Midland Railway locomotive was derailed by a landslide. This list is by no means comprehensive, but it is representative of such accidents as befell the railways during the war.

Of the other accidents and disasters much could be written, but perhaps the last few words should be said about those relating to explosives traffic. In the autumn of 1916, two accidents involving munitions trains on the Caledonian railway were remarkably free from any serious consequences. Then, on September 22nd 1917, a train of cordite and ammunition being conveyed by the LB&SCR was threatened when one of the vans caught fire. A goods inspector, C. J. Carne, bravely un-coupled the van, and with other members of staff succeeded in extinguishing the flames. For his gallantry, Mr. Carne was awarded the Albert Medal by King George V

on December 18th. Regretfully the same diligence was not exercised by his colleagues on April 18th 1918, when another LB&SCR munitions train broke in two inside Redhill Tunnel. The guard took no action for over ten minutes, and was thereby unable to prevent another freight engine, No. 541, running into the obstruction. Under the impression that nothing was amiss, the signalman allowed a train carrying naval artillery shells into the tunnel in the opposite direction. All three trains were compressed inside the bore, and despite 26 wagons being completely broken up, incredibly no fire started and none of the explosives were detonated. However, the most serious incident must be that near Bradford in the summer of 1916. A fire at the Low Moor Chemical Company was followed by an explosion, the results of which devastated Low Moor. The railway sidings were hit by a fire-ball, and the nearby gas works also exploded: at least 34 were left dead, but even today the true facts have never been made public.

By contrast with Penistone the explosion alongside the L&YR line at Low Moor on August 22nd 1916, was one of the worst civilian disasters of the war. Quite what started the fire at the chemical works south of the junction may never be known, but it has been claimed that a metal drum containing picric acid crystals was being rolled along the ground at the time.

The upper view shows the aftermath at Low Moor Junction with the branch to Heckmondwike curving away from the main Halifax-Bradford line. Over 100 wrecked wagons and vans, 30 burnt-out coaches, dozens of roof-less houses and the remains of the gas-holder all testify to the force of the explosion. Most people living nearby took shelter in the tunnel, but one lady remained in her house to tend to the stone of bread she had just put in the oven – remarkably she emerged unscathed.

The lower view is of No. 1 Signal Box after the explosion with smashed windows and broken slates being the only serious damage despite the fire-storm which swept across the adjacent tracks, consuming almost everything in its way. It is reported that at least 34 people were killed, and railway company first-aid staff were called in to render assistance. In all some 45 members of the L&YR staff received awards for gallantry because of their actions that day.
NATIONAL RAILWAY MUSEUM

Locomotives for abroad

The study of locomotive use during the period 1914-18 is a long and complex subject and though we hope to discuss it fully in a later volume, for the present we can roughly divide it into three separate areas: 1) locomotives for home use by the individual railway companies; 2) locomotives specially built for military service; and 3) locomotives requisitioned by the Government for use at home and overseas. Of these groups, we are concerned with the latter; for it presents the most interesting facets of civilian railways at war, in addition to having a direct bearing on the reduction of rail services in this country.

Railway companies had been asked by Army Railway Council as early as 1905, to provide a supply of locomotives if war should break out overseas. This request had been repeated in 1911, but in considering all the needs of the Army Railway Council (and its successor the War Railway Council), it appears as though this was the most difficult request for the railway companies to grant. It seems as though they were willing to assist, but only if a substantial compensation were paid. An alternative to this 'replacement value' compensation was proffered by J. A. F. Aspinall and H. A. Walker in 1912, whereby the companies would make available non-standard or surplus locomotives for Government service at 'book value'. The council refused to accept this

offer, seeing it only as an excuse for the companies to dump their rubbish on the War Office. Thereafter the matter lay, with little progress being made on either side.

Consequently, on the declaration of war the Army found itself without the required number of locomotives, for even the shortest of campaigns. The situation was not helped by the quick German advance on Paris, which though repulsed, saw the invaders wrecking whole sections of the French railway system as they retreated. It was therefore quite clear that not only were locomotives and drivers required, but a whole railway system would have to be created to supply the army's needs in France. It was also evident by the end of 1914 that both operating and construction corps would have to be formed, but during that first winter the whole question became as bogged down as transport in the

---

The two largest batches of locomotives sent to the ROD in France were those 8-coupled locomotives of the GCR and NER. The NER 0-8-0 locos were the Class T (LNER Q5), of which NER No. 660/ROD No. 5660 built at Darlington in June 1907 is an example. Some 50 of these engines were allocated to the ROD, and were largely employed on the heavy stone trains from the Marquise Quarries near Boulogne. The engines were returned to their owner during the first six months of 1919, with the majority being shipped on the Richborough Train Ferry.
NATIONAL RAILWAY MUSEUM

quagmire of the Western Front. The situation was far more formidable than at first envisaged, and it was not until April 1915 that the Railway Executive undertook the formation of Railway Operating Division, Royal Engineers, on behalf of the War Office.

The ROD was created by drafting a few officers from the Railway Transport Establishment, but the greatest proportion of men were recruited from the railway companies themselves. At first the division consisted of a mechanical section and an operating section, each comprised of three officers and 260 NCOs and sappers. Cecil Paget, General Superintendent of the Midland Railway was appointed Officer Commanding, later attaining the rank of Lt.-Colonel. The men were trained at Longmoor, and then sent to France where they initially took over the Belgian locomotives brought there after the fall of Belgium. The numbers grew steadily, and in July a third section was sent overseas, comprised of men drawn entirely from the LNWR. By the end of 1918 the number of British railwayman attached to the ROD was in excess of 24,000. In addition to this, eight companies of civilian platelayers numbering around 2,000 men were sent out to France from March 1917 onwards; included in the number were about 300 men who were over 60 years of age. All this indicates the substantial railway development initiated to feed the front line, carrying in replacement troops, ammunition and supplies, bringing out the maimed and wounded. The French

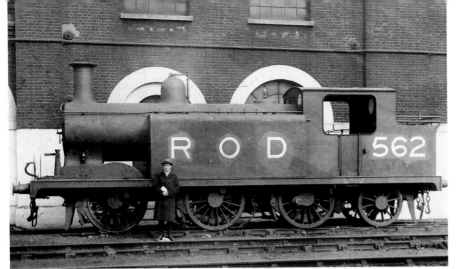

In preparation for service with the ROD, a LBSCR Class E4 No. 562 is seen at Brighton works in November 1917. Formerly called Laughton, the 0-6-2T was allocated to Tunbridge Wells shed. After being shipped to France via Dover and Calais, it was put to work on the Audruicq Ammunition Depot, along with other members of the class. They were later moved nearer to the front, but were forced to retreat when the Germans advanced on Arras. Thereafter they worked around Doullens, but after the armistice until the summer of 1919, they performed sterling duties on the Doullens-Arras direct line.
NATIONAL RAILWAY MUSEUM

network was just about shattered, especially the Nord system, of which only about 45% of the pre-war mileage remained in Allied control. Generally, it appears as though what sections of the French railways that were still running, were largely dependent on the efforts of British railwaymen. By the autumn of 1916, 490 French main-line locomotives and 54 shunting engines were in the employ of the British army, but even this was not enough. Director General of Transportation, Sir Eric Geddes, advised the War Office that to meet coming demands, at least 156 British locomotives would be needed in France. The French said the true figure was likely to be nearer 900. At the time there were 54 British locomotives working in France, and after further consultation it was reported that 2-300 locomotives and 10-20,000 wagons would be needed to support the planned British offensives the following spring. The railways were at a loss to see how this could be accomplished, even with substantial cuts in passenger services. By December 1916 the demand for main-line locomotives had

increased to 370 and the Railway Executive despatched a sub-committee to France to investigate the situation. In February it became evident that even this high number had substantially increased, when it was revealed that the British authorities in France had undertaken to provide 709 locomotives. Of these 368 had been ordered or provided, but this still left the depleted British companies with the task of finding a further 341. In addition, the War Office indicated that 81 locomotives were required for the coming Egyptian campaign. During the summer of 1917 the Locomotive Engineers sub-committee took a hard look at

the situation, which revealed that 420 engines had already been despatched to France. However, when they looked at the motive power situation at home, they discovered that a very considerable number of locomotives were stopped awaiting repair due to the lack of men and materials required to rectify them. It was evident, with 1,400 engines over and above the normal number out of service, that a serious disruption of home services would ensue that autumn. All of this posed the executive with an horrendous situation, without even considering how a further 600 engines could be released. It was a matter which could only be addressed by carrying out a physical assessment of what locomotives the companies had, and what they actually required to meet their commitments. Under a system of pooling and combined allocation,

A group of L&YR engines assembled for despatch to France are gathered round a coal stage. About one third of the total number of the L&YR locomotives supplied to the ROD are pictured here. All were Aspinall 0-6-0 tender goods engines, and were consecutively numbered from 1700 to 1731. All were built between 1889 and 1895, but despite their age, they performed valuable service in France and were greatly admired by the drivers who operated with them.
NATIONAL RAILWAY MUSEUM

the companies were able to release 123 locomotives to France, and a further 32 to the middle-East. At home the pooling resulted in considerable numbers of locomotives being loaned to other companies, with some strange workings being recorded as a result.

The following table records the total allocation of locomotives and stock loaned or sold to the Government by the British railway companies up to December 1918. The figures in parenthesis indicates where the numbers returned differs from those loaned.

Company	Locos	Wagons	Coaches
Caledonian	25	–	25
Furness	–	–	6
G&SWR	–	–	7
Great Central	33	3,267 (3,204)	20(18)
Great Eastern	43	–	–
G.N. of Scotland	–	–	31
Great Northern	26	1,000(933)	–
Great Western	73(57)	5,772(5,694)	27
Hull & Barnsley	–	–	20
L&YR	32	1,560(1,487)	–
LBSCR	12		2
LNWR	111(64)	6,370(6,119)	90(89)
LSWR	–	–	94(93)
Midland	78	6,128(6,008)	6(677)
Midland & GN Joint	–	20(19)	20
North British	25	–	–
North Eastern	50	4,545(4,448)	–
North Staffs	–	–	16
S&ECR	8	1,042(1,031)	24(23)

Concurrent with this demand for main-line and shunting locomotives, there was an additional requirement for narrow-gauge equipment to link the front lines with the supply depots in the rear. This development expanded greatly from the winter of 1916 onwards, by which time most of the roads in France and Belgium had been shelled out of existence, and as a result the supply lines were little more than a quagmire of mud and shell craters. The use of horses, motor vehicles and conventional steam locomotives was totally impractical, so to address the problem the Royal Engineers set about laying down a series of 2ft gauge lines from supply depots to the 'front'. As steam locomotives were often too heavy even in this gauge, and because exhaust steam made an excellent target for enemy artillery spotters, it was decided to employ light-weight locomotives with internal combustion engines. Accordingly a number of armour-plated 0-4-0s were purchased from a firm called Motor Rail and shipped to France in 1917 where they performed a sterling service. After the armistice many of these machines were repatriated to Britain and sold into industrial service, a use for which they were eminently suited.

Prisoners of War and Refugees

During the four and a half years of the war, and a considerable time thereafter, there was a significant traffic in those who might be termed 'the unfortunates of war': those individuals who had been ousted not only from their homes, but also their homelands. Refugees flocked to Britain throughout the war years, but of these the most numerous were Belgian. The majority arrived without any possessions, and were thus largely dependant on charity. Such aid was freely given, though it was expected that the refugees should find employment in one of the Munition works, whilst men of military age would join one of the Belgian army brigades. For both these groups, the Railway Executive was directed by the Government to provide free rail travel. In respect of Belgian railwaymen, who might be of use either here or in France, the Executive appointed a sub-committee under Mr. A. Watson of the L&YR. He placed four rooms in his Westminster offices at the disposal of the committee, and here a small

staff of railwaymen were able to direct their colleagues from Belgium into occupations suited to their training. Other sub-committees handled free travel for the refugees, and for Belgian soldiers on leave from France.

Records concerning the actual movement of prisoners of war are very scarce, and of those I consulted, none revealed any new information. However, this substantial traffic continued throughout the war years, and can be sub-divided into three categories: 1) the movement of German POWs during the war, and their eventual repatriation, 2) the recovery of British POWs after the armistice, and 3) the repatriation of any prisoner during the war years, when he was obviously ill or unfit for further military service (a little known, but widespread work carried on under the auspices of the Geneva Red Cross Commission). It is only possible to guess at the extent of POW traffic, but it emerges that the majority of German POWs were landed at Avonmouth, Southampton, Liverpool and Cardiff, and then transferred to the camps. Of those Germans who were repatriated before December 1918, it seems that the ports of Leith and Newcastle were used, as such transfers were through the

Belgian railway workers, many of them from skilled grades (ie drivers, signalmen, station masters, etc) were directed on to menial jobs on Britain's railways to replace Railwaymen who had enlisted. This often meant they were used as labourers, plate-layers, and as in this case - goods porters. In the middle of 1915 three Belgian railwaymen are seen along with their NER counterparts unloading bananas at Annfield Plain Station.
NORTH OF ENGLAND OPEN AIR MUSEUM, BEAMISH

offices of the Red Cross in Sweden. A counter-balancing arrangement was in operation for the exchange of sick British prisoners, though it seems that on their return these men were landed at Leith, Hartlepool and Hull. After the armistice, the repatriation traffic was a veritable flood and a variety of rail and ferry routes were used to convey the two-way traffic.

The following example may serve as an indication of the vast prisoner of war traffic: In 1915 a group of German prisoners were loaded into a train at Southampton. The doors of the 6-wheeled coaches had been nailed shut down one side, with half the doors on the other side similarly treated. Arriving in Wales, the captives were

marched to a camp and sorted into categories. One group of soldiers were mixed with a number of naval ratings, and they found that they all had an engineering back-ground. The group of around 50 were then sent to a camp near Carno, where they stayed for some weeks. Eventually a British major arrived, and told them that they were to be given a chance of making amends for the damage their Kaiser had done. Mystified, the men were loaded onto a train and taken on a long journey into the North of England. On arrival, they found themselves in Weardale, Co. Durham. Here they were marched over miles of barren moorland to reach an isolated village. For three and a half years the men remained here, working on a mine and quarry railway system. Most were involved in construction work, but many progressed to responsible jobs like incline brakemen, and in one case an engine driver. After the war, some decided to settle among the community who had accepted them as men, and not just the enemy, and I am indebted to one of them for recounting this story.

In the category of prisoners, we might look at another group: prisoners, not of war but of conscience. It is not widely recognized, but there were large numbers of men who refused to take up military service. A few may have been cowards, but the vast majority were men of principle and mostly belonged to religious or political organisations which refused to take sides in the issue. Prominent among these groups were the Quakers and the Jehovah's Witnesses, and despite the intense pressure put upon them to fight, most ended up in penal servitude here in Britain. Many were sent to the high security jail at Princetown, and were set to work on cultivating the harsh barren wastes of Dartmoor. By 1916, so many conscientious objectors were being sent to Dartmoor, Portland and other West Country prisons that the GWR began running special trains, the prisoners being chained for most of the journey. Interestingly, in another journey the GWR conveyed an important train with a cargo consigned to Bodmin Jail: in this instance the load was none other than the Crown Jewels which were being removed from the Tower of London for safe keeping.

Women at War

The significance of the contribution which women made to the railways is hard to comprehend in these days of female equality. However, in Edwardian Britain, the fairer sex were in no way considered equal to men so their war-time efforts are important, particularly when it is revealed that the peak number employed on the railways reached 68,801 in September 1918. Though there is no doubt that female labour was of immense value during this period, it must be realised that extreme prejudice was manifested in certain quarters. At the outbreak of war, the value of women workers was just becoming recognised, but in some industries an 'all-male' attitude still predominated. This was especially so in the railway industry, where in 1913 only 13,046 women were employed. Of these 8,482 were in 'domestic' categories, such as cleaners, waitresses, hotel staff and washer-women. Only 4,564 were employed on railway work proper, and of these most were in the clerical grades. Only in a very few instances had women progressed to more responsible positions.

All this was changed by the number of men joining the army, or called up for duties with the 'railway troops'. The labour situation became so acute by March 1915, that the Railway Executive formed a sub-committee to look at the employment of women in grades formerly occupied by men. They found that most of the clerical work, ticket

Women working on the railway were not always allocated light duties, as this picture at the Derby coal stack testifies. Some 15 ladies are pictured whilst engaged in the arduous work on May 3rd 1917, with the male crew of the depot's 25 ton crane which is being used to lift the coal skips.
NATIONAL RAILWAY MUSEUM

collection, and carriage cleaning duties could be handled by women, as could some porterage, engineering and maintenance work. Obviously, heavy duties such as engine driving and firing could not be considered, though a proposal was made that women could also be used in the quieter branch-line signal boxes. It is understood that the first woman to fill this role was at porter/signalman at Netherton Station (L&YR). As it might be expected, women excelled in clerical grades, but they also did well in other areas, for example carriage cleaning. In this regard it was found that women only managed to accomplish two thirds of the productivity of their male counterparts, but the work was of such a high standard (both internally and externally), women cleaners endeared themselves to the travelling public.

By August 1915, the committee was faced with a dilemma, for it was evident that on average three women were required to fill the roles of two men. Additionally, the percentage of women leaving after just one month's service was an alarming 42%, with a further 21% resigning after two months. A large part of the problem was that all the jobs were temporary, a fact insisted on by the National Union of Railwaymen in the protection of its members' jobs when they had enlisted. As there was no career structure, and indeed no family tradition to follow, women in the most un-rewarding jobs soon packed them in and found employment in the munitions factories where they could earn £11 per week. In times of peace a young man, say the son of an engine driver, would start with the company at the bottom; probably cleaning the very engines that one day (with effort and dedication) he would eventually fire, then drive. Such career moves were not possible to women, and thus the dedication was largely missing.

Yet, in many ways women excelled in their new careers, and a partial list of professions, is recorded at the end of 1916 as: Clerks (13,904), carriage cleaners (2,173),

workshop women (1,278), platform porters (1,098), munition workers (1,046), goods porters (901), ticket collectors (706), gate-keepers (705), engine cleaners (587), labourers (239), machinists (178), messengers (150), parcel porters (147), sack-repairers (121), painters (99), dining-car attendants (93), number-takers (79), page-girls (40), weighing-machine attendants (23), brass lacquerers (23), letter-sorters (15), signal'men' (14), horse-keepers (14), carters (12), train attendants (11), cloak-room attendants (10), luggage-room porters (10), wagon-repairers (8), hotel porters (6), harness-cleaners (6), warehouse-women (5), crockery-collectors (4), information attendants (4), ferry attendants (2), bridge-keepers (2), blind-pullers (2), flag-makers (2). There was also one woman found in each of the following occupations, gardeners, carver, printer, billiard-maker, signal cleaner/lighter, lamp room attendant, concrete-maker, canal attendant, halt-attendant, crane driver, lock-keeper, coil-maker, time-keeper, and call girl (though one suspects this was a more innocent occupation than the name might imply today!).

Another interesting group of women railway workers were those enrolled into the North Eastern Railway's police force. These railway police-women are pictured at York in 1916, and their duties were almost identical to their male counterparts, and throughout the war they acquitted themselves with distinction. Additional duties ranged from guarding railway yards to assisting the military police in the apprehension of deserters and those men who over-stayed their leave.
NATIONAL RAILWAY MUSEUM

The same returns showed that many companies had made substantial use of female labour, as for instance the GCR which had employed just 70 female clerks in 1913, and was now served by 1,526 women in that grade. Other companies maintained the prejudice, for of the 130 companies controlled by the Executive, only 68 had increased their pre-war female labour force by more than 10%. Ten of them employed none. By the end of the war men filtered back to their occupations, but in 1920 over 20,000 women were still employed in grades where their talents had become appreciated, and thus the 'male only' mould was broken. The results of this pioneering work was to become evident inside two decades, when women were to assume even greater responsibilities on Britain's railways in times of war.

Munition Works & Traffic

In view of the colossal amount of munition traffic carried in the first year of the war, a Ministry of Munitions Transport Branch was established in September 1915. The branch was sub-divided in to four sections, A. B, C and D. In turn each of these were divided into eight sub-sections, and each had an area of individual responsibility; for example, C.M. 8 was the Forwarding & Delivery dept. As such it was primarily concerned with rail traffic and all technical matters pertaining thereto, and provided advice where special facilities (like new sidings) might be required. The work was so extensive, that by February 1916, C.M.8 became the Munitions Railway Transport Branch, which was then sub-divided into eight different sections. It served various branches of the Ministry, but chiefly the, Mechanical Warfare, Gun-

ammunition Filling, Trench Warfare Supply, and Explosives Supply departments. To carry out this work, it had area offices at Newcastle, Manchester, Leeds, Birmingham, Cardiff, Bristol, London, and two in Glasgow. Most of these offices had several sub-offices, and these were nearly all based in, or near, railway stations. The role of these Area Offices was, basically, to inform the railway companies about the priority of shipments, to minimise waste journeys, arrange for sufficient wagons to be available, and to keep the Ministry fully informed on a weekly basis.

The Branch endeavoured to ensure more efficient use of resources, particularly tank wagons which were in exceptionally short supply. It also had considerable problems finding vans fitted with sorbo-rubber matting, such as those used for the transportation of volatile chemicals like nitro-glycerine and picric acid. It was evident that short distance trips, especially those around London, Birmingham, Lancashire and the

The number of shells which were daily discharged by allied guns must have reached astronomic figures, as might be understood when one considers the vast mountain of shell-cases pictured here is just a very small part of the empty cases returned to Britain for filling. The shells are seen at Doncaster Works (GNR), but similar stock-piles were seen at Derby, Gorton, Horwich, Stratford, Swindon and Wolverhampton. Many of the shells arrived back at the works in a split condition and had to be scraped, but in 1916 the GWR experts at Swindon discovered a way of brazing splits up to $1^1/_2$ inches long and thereafter the GER specialised in this avenue of the re-forming work.

NATIONAL RAILWAY MUSEUM

West Riding were making unreasonable demands on the vehicles available. Therefore they endeavoured to send consignments of less than fifteen miles distance by road: this produced tremendous savings. In Liverpool alone, over 23,000 tons of munitions was switched to the roads in October 1918. Only

The shell-cases were usually distorted to some extent, and at first the straightening was done by hand. This was a costly and time consuming process, and early in 1915 the Lancashire & Yorkshire Railway devised a shell-straightening machine which is pictured in the works at Horwich. The L&YR produced 38 of these machines which were sent to other workshops involved in munition work, in addition to the eight it produced for its own use. An example of the volume of shell-case traffic can be seen from the number of 18-pounder cases handled by the railway companies during the war which exceeded over 30 million, whilst over 3$\frac{1}{2}$ million 4.5 inch shells were attended to. All of this was in addition to the new shell-cases being turned out in the same factories – the Midland, for example, was producing around 100,000 new cases at Derby every week.
NATIONAL RAILWAY MUSEUM

by a very rigid check of vehicles, and central pooling, were the Munition Transport Officers able to keep the voluminous supplies moving.

It would be virtually impossible to document all the work of the Branch, and even to list the various rail-served munition works, shell-filling factories, and stores would be difficult. Establishments like Gretna, Erith, Woolwich, all deserve coverage, but space does not permit. Therefore, I have drawn on just a few specific examples, which serve to indicate the enormous level of this traffic. Naturally, some lines carried significantly more munition traffic than others, and whilst it might be expected on those routes leading to the embarkation ports, that on some other lines is quite surprising. Because of the potentially dangerous loads, munition trains tended to be restricted to certain routes. Generally, this led to trains being routed away from urban areas, and many took circuitous routes to reach their destination. In London it was a different matter, for the munition factories around the metropolis were forced to send this traffic through built-up areas night and day. For example, the munition factory at Hayes despatched an average of 8 trains per day, each contained upwards of 50 wagons and required double-heading. Most of these were routed via the West London lines, and worked as block trains by the L&SWR all the way to the ferry terminal at Richborough. So great was the volume of ammunition traffic on the West

London line, that it was necessary to keep the signal boxes almost continuously open. Even the tiniest of branches found

Despite the introduction of the Iron Mink standard, the number of gunpowder vans was totally inadequate for war needs between 1914-18. As will have been noted earlier, many companies converted existing vehicles into 'Special Gunpowder Vans' which were thus named in order to free them from the pending legislation concerning the movement of explosives by train. Other companies built new vans to the old designs in order to meet the immediate demand; the GNR for example produced a batch of 8-ton vans at Doncaster in August 1915, in which No. 23572 was included. The vehicles were short-lived and none were left in service by the grouping at the end of 1922.

NATIONAL RAILWAY MUSEUM

themselves carrying munitions, as exampled by the Balloch branch. This 5 mile long NBR/CR joint line from the bonny banks of Loch Lomond down to Dumbarton, conveyed countless thousands of shell casings and finished shells that were produced in the district. On some main lines, significant problems were encountered by the sheer volume of this traffic, including the section of the Caledonian Railway where it passed into England. So great was the flow of munition traffic between Gretna and Carlisle, that the company was unable to cope. This was reported back to the Railway Executive and within three weeks the Ministry of Munitions had approved, and provided £60,000 for widening the line between Floriston and Rockliffe.

Another major form of traffic governed by the Branch, was that of picric acid. This was a major constituent in most explosives, and

our pre-war needs had been largely supplied by the Essen Dye-works in Germany. When these chemicals became un-available the dye-works in Britain were unable to cope, so in 1915-6 the Government provided resources to set up new plants in the textile producing areas. One of the leading dye experts of the time, Major L. B. Holliday was released from war service to establish a picric plant and munitions works at Bradley near Huddersfield. The Ministry of Munitions were persuaded to lay in a two-mile system of sidings, connected to the LNWR line, and operated (like most other munition sites) with fire-less locos. Holliday seized the opportunity, and built a large dye-works on an adjoining site at Deighton, laying in more sidings to serve it. Alas, his unauthorised scheme was discovered and the Government refused to pay for the additional work.

The role of the Railway Workshops

From the very outset of the war in August 1914, it became evident that the necessities of the conflict would quickly out-strip the capacity for producing the required supplies. This placed the government in an awkward position, which could only be addressed by the utilisation of civilian factories for war-production. In this regard, the railway companies became directly involved in the manufacture of a variety of supplies for the armed forces. The work at first was low-key, and of such a nature as to not have too great an effect on routine business in the various locomotive works and carriage and wagon shops: constructions of special military needs, like the ambulance or armoured trains being in effect, just normal railway work.

The Railway Executive initially agreed to the use of railway workshops, on the proviso that it did not materially affect the companies' ability to fulfil its needed work of the repair and replacement of railway equipment. Happily the leading companies agreed that they could assist, and in the autumn of 1914 the workshops at Ashford, Barassie, Brighton, Cowlairs, Crewe, Darlington, Derby, Doncaster, Duckinfield, Earlstown, Eastleigh, Gateshead, Glasgow, Gorton, Horwich, Lancing, Newton Heath, St. Rollox, Stratford, Swindon, Temple Mills, Wolverton and York began work for the war effort. The first order was for the ambulance trains which we will discuss later, to be followed on September 2nd by a request for 12,250 stretchers. A fortnight later, an order was received for 5,000 general service wagons (road). This figure was then increased to 6,000, whilst the stretcher order was more than doubled by the end of the year. Orders were received for the conversion of 500, 10 ton covered goods vans to military use, with supplies to begin reaching Government depots by November. Soon the workshops were entering the field of munitions and armament manufacture, and the resulting pressure this caused was referred to the Railway Executive.

In October 1914, a Railway War Manufactures Sub-Committee was established to regulate the flow of this work, and where possible make better use of existing facilities in the different workshops. The names of the members of that committee testify to its importance, for it was comprised of such notable figures as: Henry Fowler, C. H. Dent, H. N. Gresley, George Hughes, G. J. Churchward and C. J. Bowen Cooke; if this were not enough, the group was later to include A. J. Hill, P. Drummond, W. Pickersgill, J. G. Robinson and Vincent Raven. the sub-committee had to decide three pre-requisites before agreeing to the acceptance of any war work at the railway workshops, these being: Could such work be done, a) under present conditions, b) if railway repair work were curtailed, or c) if extra plant were laid down with the government supplying such plant or the capital for its cost? Option a) was almost impossible because of the number of railway employees who had enlisted in the armed forces, though the Government agreed to release such men if they were willing to return. Many did, but even so, it was largely options b) and c) which had to be adopted.

By the end of the year, around 31 companies were actively involved in Government production or related sub-contract work, though strange to relate, this number had not substantially increased at

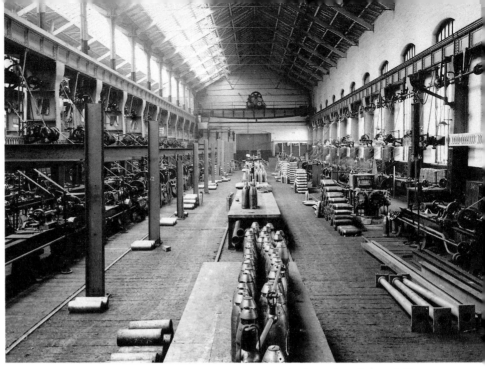

As indicated in the previous chapter, shell manufacture assumed phenomenal proportions in the railway workshops from 1915 onwards. In addition to all the re-forming work, thousands of new cases, fuses, adaptors and gaines were produced. The NER at Darlington turned out around $1^1/_2$ million complete shells during the war, and even the little L&Y did considerable munitions work at Horwich. Over 142,000 fuses were made, of Mk 101, Mk 102 and Mk 103 varieties. Shells up 13.5 inch were manufactured in the works, though this view in the erecting shop shows newly produced shells of a smaller calibre.
NATIONAL RAILWAY MUSEUM

the end of the war. It is difficult to cover all the aspects of war production at the railway workshops, for the official list of the different items produced between August 1914 December 1918 amounts to no less than a 121 page document. Much of the early work was, however, still closely related to the peace-time activities of the workshops and the involvement therefore caused little hardship to companies. It became the rule that if a particular works had spare capacity, or could achieve such capacity by temporarily postponing less urgent work,

then it would accept the Government orders. Unfortunately, this position changed dramatically in 1915, when the supply of shells to the Western Front was found to be totally inadequate. Following the catastrophic attack at Lislie on May 4th 1915, the *Times* recorded that the British failure was due to a lack of high explosives to level the enemy positions – compared to the French, whom it seemed, were in the position of being able to fire 276 rounds per gun. The matter was raised in Parliament on May 14th, and the following day the Railway Executive Committee were asked if some of its workshops could be turned over for the necessary production. On June 8th 1915, Royal Assent was given for the formation of the Ministry of Munitions, and within days of its inception, orders for machining 2,250 shells a week were issued to the Executive. The principal capacity was to be provided by seven companies: the GCR, GER, GNR, GWR, LNWR, L&YR and NER, who in turn would distribute the work around their various workshops. In addition, the GWR was asked to cast some 2,000 6 inch high-explosive shells every week.

Even though the Government assisted by releasing over 2,650 skilled machinists from the armed forces, the strain imposed by all this work was creating considerable problems which could not be addressed simply by recruiting female labour. Essential maintenance of the railways began to suffer as result. The situation had become so extreme by April 1916 that the Chairman of the Board of Trade was forced to write to the Railway Executive, stating:-

"If the railway service is impeded, or if any accident occurs owing to rolling stock getting out of condition in consequence of the railway workshops being engaged in the manufacture of munitions of war, I must hold the Railway Executive Committee responsible".

Such strong words were a severe indictment on the Executive, but secretly it must have come as a relief to many operating departments which faced the severest crisis in motive power and rolling stock availability in the history of railways.

The Executive could do nothing other

than comply with the wishes of the BoT, and stated that such work on munitions that was being carried on would only be done if it were not prejudicial to the safe running of the railways. However, it was found, that by now most of the machine work was being done by women and girls who, having learned the job thoroughly, were more suited to long repetative orders than their male counterparts. The railway companies therefore continued to accept this work, but added that they must be allowed to refuse such orders as would delay the essential work on railway matters; and if they refused an order on these grounds, they would only take on such work on the receipt of a direct command from the BoT, who it turn would have to accept any consequences that might befall the railways as a result of vital maintenance being forsaken in preference to that for the military.

In the main, it was a marriage of convenience, and somehow the wishes of all the interested parties were met, this largely being at the expense of routine and non-essential maintenance, which was repeatedly deferred. In doing this, the railways were only postponing what they would inevitably have to face, and the Railway Executive made this point in no uncertain terms. In return the Government agreed to compensate the companies, and make good any losses they sustained by delaying their own work on behalf of the war effort. That is not to say railway maintenance did not take place in the war years, of course it did, though on a greatly reduced scale. Perhaps the greatest single indicator of the effect that war had on routine railway work, is the pathetically low number of new locomotives and stock turned out between 1915 and 1918. In view of the sheer quantity of goods the railway companies produced, it is not possible to list what each of the works did, but the following list of the railways involved in war work is of interest.

Barry
Brecon & Merthyr
Cambrian
Caledonian
Furness
Glasgow & Sth.
 Western
Great Central
Great Eastern
Great Northern
G.N. of Scotland
Great Western
Highland
Hull & Barnsley
Lancashire &
 Yorkshire
London & North Western

London & Sth.
 Western
London Brighton
 & Sth. Coast
Metropolitan
Meytropolitan District
Midland
Midland & GNR Joint
North British
North Eastern
North Staffordshire
Rhymney
South East & Chatham
Taff Vale
5 Irish railway works and
27 private railway
workshops

The above list is not totally representative, for during the period concerned many other railway workshops were used for war-production, though in such cases the work was either of a limited quantity, or was undertaken sub-contract from another company. For example, the engineering facilities of the Maryport & Carlisle Railway were put at the disposal of the LNWR for a while, and later much work was undertaken there as sub-contract for Samuel Pearson & Co during their construction of the Gretna Munitions factory. However, whether a railway workshop was engaged in war-work or not, it can be safely said that all such facilities were worked to their maximum capacity during those troubled years.

As the numbers of railway vans required for service overseas grew, it became evident that the ROD could no longer rely on the requisition of goods vehicles from the home railways. Accordingly, from late 1916 onwards, a series of specially designed 20-ton vans were ordered from a variety of workshops around the country. The view here shows the 'assembly line' production of vans at the LB&SCR's wagon works.

Ambulance Trains

The value of ambulance trains was first recognised in the American Civil War, and their use in Atlanta, Georgia was portrayed in the epic film 'Gone with The Wind'. Britain's first such trains evolved in the South African War (1899-1902), when the British Red Cross Committee ordered the 'Princess Christian Hospital Train' from the Birmingham Railway, Carriage & Wagon Co., and had it shipped out to the Natal. Meanwhile, the War Office asked the L&SWR to adapt a five coach train to serve the wounded arriving back at Southampton. Impressed with its efficiency, the War Railway Council retained the L&SWR train and asked the LNWR to prepare plans for the conversion of ordinary bogie coaching stock into nine-coach ambulance trains: in turn the railway

An Ambulance Train being loaded at Doullens during the First World War
COPYRIGHT: IMPERIAL WAR MUSEUM. COURTESY: DR. BRIAN ROBERTSON

companies agreed to supply them in the following proportions: LNWR, three: GCR, GWR, and Midland two each; the GER, L&SWR and L&YR would each make one complete train.

When war broke out, all twelve were to be sent to Eastleigh to join the Red Cross and L&SWR ambulance trains, providing a total of fourteen such trains for use by the army. Correspondingly, the Royal Navy had none, as pre-war planning had centred largely on the use of hospital ships, and the large naval hospitals at Chatham, Portsmouth and Plymouth. The weaknesses in the Admiralty's planning soon became apparent, and on August 6th 1914 a request was sent to the LNWR carriage works at Wolverton to prepare five trains for the Navy in addition to those under construction for the Army.

The first wounded soldiers were landed at Southampton on August 24th, and because none of the new ambulance trains were yet available, it fell to using the old L&SWR train (supplemented with six coaches), in moving all

the injured to hospital at Netley. Later on that same day, the GCR train arrived and was immediately put to work. As hospitals around Southampton became over-crowded, the first ambulance train to take patients off the L&SWR system was No. 6 (supplied by the L&YR); on August 29th it transported 187 men to Well Hall Station on the South Eastern & Chatham. By 4 pm the following day, all twelve new trains were in use, but his was insufficient for the growing flow of the wounded, sick, and mental patients reaching Southampton and Dover. Four more trains were supplied in January, but meanwhile five emergency ambulance trains were formed to transport sitting cases. By February the allocation of the trains was: four ambulance, two emergency at Dover; and at Southampton; twelve ambulance, two emergency trains; the Red Cross train went to France, whilst the L&SWR set and one emergency train were allocated to the Navy.

By May 1915 the War Office intimated it needed more trains, for use both at home and overseas. To resolve how these needs could be

Ambulance train No. 29 on display prior to entering War Department service. These trains were somewhat smaller than the 16-coach continental ambulance trains, as the home trains could complete a round-trip to even the furthest destination inside 48 hours. Accordingly they did not require the same facilities as those used on the Continent where the trains might take several days to reach one of the channel ports used to repatriate the wounded.
M. ELTHAM COLLECTION

met, the Railway Executive formed two sub-committees, one for 'home' trains, and another for those needed on the continent. The home committee under H. Holmes (L&SWR), addressed the problem at once, and by the end of the war a total of twenty army ambulance trains had been supplied by just seven companies. A Continental Sub-committee was established under the chairmanship of F. H. Dent, of the South Eastern & Chatham. Along with H. D. Earl, Carriage Superintendent of the LNWR, and A. J. Hill, CME to the GER, Dent visited France to discuss the precise requirements with officials of the Surgeon-General's staff. Accordingly, designs were prepared for a standard train of sixteen vehicles, and in the years which followed British railway companies supplied a total of 30 such trains for use by the British Army, in France, Egypt and Mesopotamia. A

Ambulance train 42 featured in 1917/18 along with the British and American nurses who manned these trains. The station has not been identified, but one of the nurses in the view was a relation of fellow railway historian Oliver Carter who would welcome more informationon the picture!
O. F. CARTER COLLECTION

further 19 ambulance trains were built for use by the American Army in France. In all, for British and American use overseas, the railway companies supplied a total of 822 ambulance coaches, of which only 30 were non-bogie stock.

Repatriated casualties were conveyed by ambulance trains to over 196 receiving stations, from where they were taken by road to hospitals near their homes, or those which had the special facilities to care for their injuries. Notification of ambulance train

Interior of train No. 37 showing one of the nine main cars. The three-tiered bunks show the numbers who might be conveyed thus, with the upper-bunks usually being reserved for the most serious cases. These bunks were never disturbed, but the two lower sets of bunks could be folded to provide comfortable seats on which the patients might lounge during the day. The idea of folding bunks/seats was instituted by the Railway Executive, but its design is attributed to F. W. Marillier, Carriage Manager of the GWR.

NATIONAL RAILWAY MUSEUM

movements were often printed in the press, and at major railway stations it became practice for local people to bring gifts of food, flowers and newspapers for the wounded. Regretfully, many of the wounded died en-route, whilst others had to be removed to a hospital when the motion of the train opened up their wounds. The ambulance trains were treated with priority, but it was impossible to prevent them suffering problems which inevitably befall most railway movements. The most unfortunate incident was suffered by men of the Northumberland Fusiliers and the Durham Light Infantry, on May 3rd 1915. While bound for hospital in Aberdeen, Train No. 9 became derailed just south of Kendal causing severe problems which necessitated at least one patient being removed to the Cumberland Infirmary in Carlisle. Generally, most of the workings arrived safely at their destination, and by the end of the war over five million soldiers, sailors and airmen had been conveyed by train to various hospitals in Britain.

By contrast the interiors of naval ambulance trains were considerably different, as the Navy preferred the use of folding canvas cots to stretchers. These were much easier to negotiate around the narrow passages and companion-ways of HM ships, and could be lifted vertically (as though the patient were standing) through hatches – particularly those on submarines. Once placed in a cot, the patient would normally remain cocooned within until he reached hospital. On the hospital trains, these cots were suspended from the roof by a series of tier brackets.

ROYAL NAVAL MUSEUM, PORTSMOUTH

Demobilisation

As the war ground remorselessly on through 1917, and in spite of the continued movement of men to the 'front', the Railway Executive began to make plans for the eventual demobilisation of the troops. Though these plans were purely anticipatory, it seemed that following the American involvement, the allies would surely win – it was all a question of how long Germany would hold out.

The Executive Committee's plans were made personally by a group of General Managers, in recognition of the immense importance attached to the work by the War Office. The Committee had to address itself to a number of aspects of the demobilsation, which was split into two distinct parts – those men serving overseas, and those based at home. The War Office divided all its men into three categories, and by these groups they would be demobilised. First of these were the demobilisers; men who, in either military or civilian roles, would fill essential duties in the demobilisation of those who followed. Second were the 'Pivot-men'; men who would be employed in key occupations concerned with the reconstruction of Britain, a group in which coal miners, architects, builders, engineers and railwaymen were included. Finally, there came the demobilisation of 'other troops', including those of the Dominion forces.

Plans were drawn up to demobilise the troops through twenty Special Area Centres in

---

Troops disembark in the North-east in April 1919, having been conveyed there direct from Hamburg. The unit was to be sent to the large barracks at Catterick, and later disbanded as the men were sent to demobilisation centres around the country. In all this work, the railways played an important role, though from places like Newcastle, Hartlepool, Leith and Hull there was a considerable return traffic as the repatriation programme got underway.
KIRKLEES MUSEUMS & LIBRARIES

Britain, each centre representing a number of counties. Men who lived in, or intended to take up residence in those counties would be sent to that centre, regardless of which regiment or ship they had served in. For example, men from Cumberland, Lancashire, Westmorland and the Isle of Man would be sent to Area No. 3, for which the LNWR station at Prees Heath near Shrewsbury was the transportation point.

Moving Home Command troops to the centres was considered to be a relatively easy task, but it was an entirely different situation concerning those overseas. Endeavouring to sort them out into the respective areas, and provide trains at the reception ports would be no small matter. The Executive reported its concerns to the War Office, and between them they envisaged a scheme which, as planned, promised an even sweeter operation than the mobilisation. Troops were to be sent to rest camps in France, each camp corresponding with a demobilisation centre in Britain. When they were fully rested, and sufficient numbers had been collected, whole contingents would

Meanwhile not all of Britain's armed forces were allowed to return home, but even for those who were to remain in the services there were very generous leaves granted from the end of of 1918. Of the larger leave traffic, the bulk originated from naval depots in Scotland with Leith and Invergordon being the two principal centres from where men would head home. Ships were sent to one of the two establishments for re-fitting and the men would get up to a month's leave, and special trains were laid on for their benefit. The scene here at Invergordon station at the end of the year pictures one group of ratings who will be home for Christmas.
ROYAL NAVAL MUSEUM., PORTSMOUTH

be repatriated to the specified 'centre'. Where possible there would be through working from France to England, but it is not certain whether this would have involved the Richborough Train Ferry.

It was an admirably conceived scheme, and after the armistice it worked well for several weeks. Thereby about 20,000 men per day were returned from France, and along with 5-6,000 per day from British camps, they were conveyed to the area demobilisation centres. However, the transfer of men from camps in the Home Command was less orderly than had been anticipated. Each Area Command released about 500 men each day, issuing them all with a travel warrant. As there were no special travel arrangements for these men, the un-regulated flow caused considerable

difficulties for the railway companies who were unable to anticipate the demand for trains. In order to meet this situation, the Executive established 'railway assembly points' and demanded that, on release, all Home Command troops should first make their way to the one nearest their barracks. From these points, special trains were run on specific days of the week to the various centres, thereby moving the released men back to their home areas with the least possible inconvenience.

All went well with the front-line demobilisation, until the French authorities decided they could not tolerate the railway congestion imposed by sending men to rest camps for sorting. It announced that thereafter 'French Railways would only convey British troops to the nearest port' – a laughable fact when one considers that most of the French lines were only being worked thanks to the involvement of British railwaymen and locomotives. However, the War Office acceded to the demand, and thereafter the grouping of soldiers had to be done in England, with 'Area Centre trains' from the reception ports often being run in three or more parts to coincide with troop-ship arrivals. In this respect it

became necessary to run trains to each area camp from Tilbury, Southampton, Plymouth, Dover and ten other ports, so it is easy to appreciate how complicated the new arrangements came to be.

The demobilisation of the Colonial and Dominion forces was a different matter, for owing to the lack of available troop-ships, these men could not be repatriated to their home country immediately. Therefore they were established in camps near to their eventual embarkation points: Liverpool, Glasgow and

Unfortunately, not everyone returned as at least 16,000,000 men from all the countries involved lost their lives. The vast majority were buried in the great anonymous cemeteries of France, but some were returned for burial in their home towns. These men were usually those who died in hospital after being returned to Britain, or senior officers who were shipped back from France. The details of this Military Funeral at Dewsbury in 1918 are not recorded, though from the ceremony it might be assumed that it was either a senior officer or a soldier who had distinguished himself in battle.
KIRKLEES MUSEUMS & LIBRARIES

Avonmouth for the Canadians: Southampton for the Australians, New Zealanders and South Africans etc. In putting these men into camps, the Government felt it would like to allow as many of those who wanted, opportunity to see the motherland. Free warrants were issued, almost for unlimited travel, and various industries were instructed to welcome these 'colonials' and show them British methods of working. The railways were considerably helpful in this regard, and many of these soldiers underwent periods of training on British railways, in the hope that it might help them find jobs back home. Others, studied British transport methods with an eye to improving arrangements in their own industries. Fishermen from Newfoundland went to Peterhead and Aberdeen, to witness methods employed in the Scottish industry. South African fruit farmers went to Covent Garden to look at the market there, then they looked at steam heated railway vans with a view to using these to import their crops to Britain. It was much the same with sheep farmers from Australia and New Zealand who envisaged the use of refrigerated ships and railways in the supply of meat for Smithfield. In all these regards the railway companies cooperated fully, and nurtured the first seeds of what grew into a valuable import trade.

As far as the railways were concerned, demobilisation began on December 9th 1918. From here-on, the companies handled everything from men to machines, and from horses to tanks. On behalf of the War Office, they even accepted returned great-coats which could be handed in for a £1 gratuity at any railway station. By May 1919 only six of the Area Camps were left open; namely, Aldershot, Crystal Palace, Fovant, Prees Heath, Purfleet and Ripon. At the start of the following year Purfleet was the only one remaining, though Prees Heath and Fovant were converted into rest camps for men returning from overseas via Southampton, Plymouth and Liverpool docks. But this is not the end of the story, defeated Germany would now face a humiliating experience at the hands of the Allies in their terms for peace. This was followed by reparations resulting in the economic collapse of Germany. Next came a world wide slump, international labour troubles and the collapse of money markets all of which led up to the great Depression. In turn the world re-armed in preparation for the next stage of conflict!

BETWEEN THE WARS

Worn out and suffering! *The ravages of extensive use during the war years of 1914-18, a number of pieces of railway infrastructure required urgent attention. One such example was the Woodhead Tunnel on the GCR route between Manchester and Sheffield. Seeking to address the problems caused by continual damage from sulphurous smoke fumes, the LNER decided to electrify the line. Regrettably the advent of World War II would prevent this, at the cost of a completely new tunnel having to be constructed later. In 1936 an ex-GCR 4-6-0 Class B7/2 heads in at the Dunford Bridge end.* D. IBBOTSON

Battered and Bruised

It is hard to present a complete picture of the state the railways had degenerated to when the armistice was signed between Germany and the Allied and Associated Powers in a railway coach at Compiägne on November 11th 1918. Ironically that same coach would be used 22 years later when Hitler made the French sign their armistice at the very same location on June 22nd 1940, but in the meantime the railways of Europe would face substantial changes. Understandably, the battle damaged lines of mainland Europe were bound to be rebuilt, and in their rebuilding vast improvements would be made, with many of the new technological innovations of the period being incorporated. Money for reconstruction was at a premium, but nevertheless the continental railways benefited substantially. The same was hardly true of railways in Britain which, battered and bruised by five years of war, were at one of the lowest ebbs in their history. We have already discussed how much essential maintenance work had been deferred during the war years, resulting in a backlog of work in every department, particularly permanent way, locomotives and rolling stock. Whilst work progressed to address these issues in other European countries, there was a massive shortage of funds, material and manpower affecting proposals for a similar rehabilitation of British railways. Steel was in particularly short supply and, despite the creation of a national Forestry Commission, timber was even scarcer. What few materials

The levels of military and civilian traffic on the railway during the war years has already been commented upon, but few may realise that considerable work in connection with military projects continued for a number of years yet to come. One such example was the munitions factory at Gretna, where large numbers of special trains ran throughout the early 1920s carrying workers to and from places like Carlisle, Brampton, Longtown, Annan and Dumfries.
AUTHOR'S COLLECTION

that were available for reconstruction work in the post war period, were generally poor or of inferior quality.

The shortage of manpower was also becoming a critical factor by the end of 1919, with huge losses being sustained amongst the railway servants who had undertaken military service. For example, of the 18,957 railwaymen who died because of the war, the GWR alone lost nearly two and a half thousand. The same sort of loss ratio was echoed amongst the other pre-grouped companies, but there were other factors to be considered as well. For every railwayman killed in action, at least another three were so badly injured as to make them unable to resume their normal careers, shell-shock and gas wreaking the greatest havoc. Hundreds more railway employees, particularly in the railway workshops and permanent way departments were prematurely aged by the strain of the excessive work load. Coupled with this was the postwar release of many of the women workers who had been employed for the 'duration', although a number were retained for secretarial and clerical posts which had previously been male jobs. Poverty (the railwaymen's incomes had never been very high) and privation were also noted by the rail unions to be 'increasing greatly, no doubt a direct consequence of the war'. On top of all this came the terrible epidemic of 1919, Spanish influenza, which claimed more victims world-wide than had died in the Great War which had just ended. It went through the railways like a plague, sweeping high and low. In just one week the LNWR lost 421 employees (or members of their families) including the General Manager Sir Guy Calthrop (aged 44).

Life on the railways was bedevilled with a number of major problems through the three years that followed the war, but remarkably, it was not attended by the same level of disasters that were witnessed at the end of the Second World War. Though there had been a spate of horrific railway accidents during the war years (see pages 38-40), the period leading up to the

Grouping was relatively free of major incidents. The exception being at Abermule on the Cambrian Railway on January 26th 1921. However, as this was an accident caused by human error, it can not be attributed to the lack of maintenance which caused so many of the post-WWII disasters. One thing that is noticeable, however, are the number of accidents which occurred after the Grouping, where it is clear that the lack of investment in new equipment (during the period 1914-1923) was a contributory factor. Nowhere was this more true than the case of signalling and train protection, as a study of Railway Inspectorate Reports will reveal. It is not that work was not being authorised, it was, but there was a genuine funding gap which was hard to bridge. For example, between 1919 and 1920 the GWR

From February 1919 onwards there was a general clamour for improved working conditions which led to a railway strike commencing on September 26th. Some railwaymen refused to join and the companies could keep skeleton services operational, thanks to the voluntary services of members of the public - particularly students. This led to difficulties with men becoming marked as 'black-legs' because they did not join in the strike. For most it was a case of 'being sent to Coventry' but some of the reprisals were of a very extreme nature. The second time when this situation arose was during the General Strike of 1926, which lasted from May 4th to 14th. In Ireland a number of extreme actions were witnessed, including this tragic deliberate derailment at Dromiskin where two men were killed and many more injured. M. ELTHAM/TIMES COLLECTION

After many years of hard wear and exceptionally (and abnormally) heavy traffic, the railways emerged from the war in a considerably run-down condition. Coupled with this came the years of deferred maintenance, railway strikes, a general trade depression and, more than all else, fierce competition from road traffic of all kinds. The depression ran between 1929 and 1934, peaking in 1932 with a staggering effect on the railways including a substantial reduction in heavy mineral traffic. Orders for replacement stock were halted, and many existing engines were laid up due to a lack of work. Typical of the motive power scene just prior to the Grouping is this re-built Dean convertible 4-4-0 seen at Reading in 1922. THE LATE M.W. EARLEY, AUTHOR'S COLLECTION.

had been authorised to construct over 81 miles of new railways, but very little of this had actually been commenced by the end of 1920.

Yet, despite all the great difficulties being faced by the railway management, the demand for travel was continuing apace. The summer of 1919 saw a mass exodus to the seaside towns, so much so that even small resorts witnessed phenomenal numbers of trains. For example,

the little NER station at Withernsea received 90 special trains on the August Bank Holiday Monday that year, in addition to its normal scheduled services. The years 1920 and 1921 were just as busy, with the public's insatiable demand for travel having been widened now that men, who had previously never travelled much beyond their home town, had been carried all over Europe in their military service.

It was not, however, all doom and gloom as the companies quickly endeavoured to resume normality. For example on February 3rd 1919, a cross-channel service was reinstated, and in the same year the GWR introduced cheap day returns. By 1920 the L&YR, LBSCR, SECR and GER were reintroducing long distance excursions. The main express locomotive developments of the year immediately prior to grouping was the introduction of Pacific engine types by the NER and GNR. The type had hitherto just been the GWR's sole 4-6-2 Great Bear, but it was the LNER who were to make such a great impact with the introduction of the type, represented here by doyen of the A1 class No.1470 Great Northern *pictured at Doncaster in GNR livery.* LNER OFFICIAL PICTURE, AUTHOR'S COLLECTION

Thomas Cook & Co. did a roaring trade to the middle classes, selling inclusive railway/steamer trips to France and Belgium. Many of the people availing themselves of these trips were officers going back to view the battlefield areas with their families, whilst others were widows of men who had fallen in battle. Local travel had also widened, and with the movement of labour directed to new employment during the war years, a new type of traffic (the blue-collar commuter) had been developed. At the end of 1921 the GWR, the largest of the pre-Grouped companies, handled 7.2 million passengers. Close on their heels were the LNWR and Midland, each with 7.1 million. In goods movement, it was again the GWR who came top, carrying 4.2 million tons of freight, followed by the Midland, NER and LNWR in second, third and fourth positions respectively. The premier place for the company handling longer hauls, calculated on a tons-miles basis, was achieved by the Midland. However, a worrying trend as far as freight traffic was concerned was a general shrinkage of the railway companies' road haulage capacity. True, many horse-drawn vehicles were being replaced by motor vehicles, but as we shall see later the railways were not adequately responding to the number of small operators setting up in competition against them.

In view of competition from motor lorry, tram and omnibus, coupled with the inherent problems stemming from over-use and underfunding, the railways were in dire need of assistance. Would this be forthcoming under the terms agreed by the Government, or would they fail to fully honour their promises as many companies suspected? Even before the war ended a Select Committee of Parliament (detailed in the next section) had been formed to discuss the future of the railways, but more worrying noises were being made. Initiatives which the railway companies were putting forward met stiff opposition from the Railway Executive Committee, in safety terms alone this was highly contentious. For example, the crazy situation arose where one Government agency was refusing funding for safety improvements to track and signalling which another Government department was ordering the railway companies to carry out. This situation, as well as the others, simply could not be allowed to continue. The long period of uncertainty brought about when Winston Churchill advocated the nationalisation of the railways whilst delivering a speech in Dundee at the end of 1918, had to be finally resolved - one way or the other!

The Grouping

The House of Commons Select Committee on Transport had been appointed on August 16th 1918 to look at the role the railways would play once hostilities were ended. This no doubt emanated from the changes in ideology that all wars bring about, including the then fashionable theories on industrial democracy, rationalisation and promotion of efficiency that were sweeping the country. The idea of a return to prewar ways, as far as the railways were concerned, went very much against the grain of this thinking and many people within the industry could see benefits from mergers between certain companies. Certainly, the national control of the railways had introduced a number of areas where better working practices could be achieved, along with much needed economies. This was in stark contrast with philosophies of the Victorian era when there had been an almost paranoid fear of railway amalgamation leading to the creation of monopolies, as these were considered to be detrimental to both the national economy and social good. This thinking was occasionally interspersed with more liberal views on mergers, but even so the Board of Trade frequently railed against them even in the more 'enlightened' political periods. Even logical, and expediently essential mergers between companies like the London Chatham & Dover and the South Eastern were strongly resisted in certain quarters. However, not only was there political and operational elements to consider, but also the view of the shareholders, many of whom would suffer substantial losses if mergers went ahead.

On November 14th the Select Committee presented its report, but instead of a series of recommendations, it merely stressed the alternatives which were:-

1. Further amalgamation of the railway companies as a step towards unification.
2. Unification accompanied by private ownership and commercial management.
3. Unification by means of Nationalisation.

If the third option was chosen, the committee suggested that this would be followed by:-

a. The establishment of Government Department to manage the railways,
b. Constitution of a Management Board not directly represented in Parliament.
c. Leasing the system to one or more companies.

Despite its impressive reputation, the Great Western was in fact the second smallest of the Big Four, with a network of just 3,703 miles - less than half that of the LMS. However, unlike its competitors where, frequent 'pre-Grouping allegiances' served to mar a cohesive development, the GWR had few such problems by comparison, This was probably due to the fact that it absorbed, rather than merged with its constituents, and more quickly imposed its image and working practices over what were, in effect, treated merely as subsidiary companies. The miscellany of locomotives acquired at the grouping, were very soon scrapped and replaced by standard Swindon types. One of the least aesthetically pleasing productions to come out of Swindon was the 'streamlined' No. 5005 Manorbier Castle.*
BRITISH RAILWAYS WESTERN REGION

It was left to the Government to chose which option they would adopt, but it does not appear clear as to whether in fact they had made up their mind when the Ministry of Transport Act was passed in 1919. Initially conceived as the Ministry of Ways and Communications, the MoT was an amalgamation of the former Roads Board and the Railway Division of the Board of Trade. Appointed as its first Minister, was Sir Eric C. Geddes who had enjoyed a meteoric rise to his new position from the minor position of Claims Agent on the NER in 1904. By 1911 he had already become Deputy General Manager and tipped to succeed Sir A. Kaye Butterworth on his retirement. However, the NER released Geddes for War Service in 1915 where he became Deputy Director-General of Munition Production. Inside 18 months he had become Inspector General of Transportation in France, before becoming First Lord of the Admiralty in May 1917. After the cessation of hostilities, the War Cabinet appointed him in complete charge

of its 'Demobilisation Co-ordination'. Geddes was faced with a number of issues, with all sides calling for various types of reform. For example, the Railway Nationalisation Society pressed for nothing other than the complete unification of the railways, whilst railway managers like Arthur Watson of the L&YR (a close friend of Geddes) was writing long articles against the proposals in newspapers like the Manchester Guardian. Also vociferous in their concerns about the future were, quite understandably, the rail unions. More noticeable amongst these was the Associated Society of Locomotive Engineers & Firemen and Railway Clerks Association. As a consequence, in 1920, the Ministry proposed that representatives of the workforce be appointed to the new railway boards on their formation.

When Geddes new Ministry started drafting legislation, it was evident that he could not please everyone, particularly as the attitude against complete nationalisation was hardening.

The smallest company, the Southern, only had 2,200 route miles, but many of these were amongst the most extensively worked in the country. Heavy suburban traffic out of London placed exceptional demands on steam services, and it is not surprising that the Southern were quick to develop its electrification programme. Yet, coupled with this was a desire to dispose of anything which did not lend itself to standardisation, most notably their only narrow gauge line, the Lynton & Barnstaple Rly. (pictured top), which was closed in 1935. In standardising, the Southern adopted the ex-LSWR 600v DC third-rail electric system instead of the 6,600v AC overhead wires of the LBSCR which was phased out in 1929. Unfortunately, with electrification, there was also a serious deterioration in the standards of passenger comfort due to the rough riding EMU sets. Despite the erstwhile efforts of the company's publicity department, Southern electrics were irreverently nicknamed "Southern Epileptics". Despite the poor ride and a resultant adverse affect on the track, the services were gradually improved and expanded upon. The undated view below shows a 6PUL set on a down Eastbourne working along the 'Quarry' line. BOTH AUTHOR'S COLLECTION

The more favoured option was towards a system of unification based on a smaller number of private companies, but without union representation on the boards as this proposal had been objected to by both the Railway Companies' Association and the unions. A further change was the abolition of the proposals for a Scottish company, which had been strongly opposed north of the border because it was felt that the new national wage standards would raise Scottish costs disproportionately. What came was the proposal for four companies, viz:-

1. A southern group, comprised of the LSWR, LBSCR, SER, LC&DR railways and a number of minor subsidiaries or joint lines and stations.

2. A western group, comprised of the GWR, Barry, Cambrian, Cardiff, Rhymney, Taff Vale railways and the Alexandra Docks & Railways Co. Once again, these main constituents would be grouped together with a number of minor subsidiaries or joint lines and stations.

3. A North-western, Midland and West Scottish Group, into which the Caledonian, Furness, G&SWR, Highland L&YR, LNWR, Midland and North Staffordshire companies would be merged, along with, once again, a number of minor subsidiaries or joint lines and stations.

4. The North Eastern & East Scottish Group was the final proposal, and would include the GCR, GER, GNR, Great North of Scotland, Hull & Barnsley and NER undertakings, with the now usual collection of minor subsidiaries or joint lines and stations.

These proposals were possibly a good compromise, but there were a number of anomalies that were not sufficiently addressed, with lines from one company penetrating well into the territory of another. A good example of this might be found with the LNER system serving west coast ports like Silloth and Mallaig. It was this type of illogical consequence of the proposed Grouping that caused much complaint, and in 1920 a Times leader questioned 'why the Government had not caused a series of areas or territories to be created and the leasing of these to the operating companies as has been achieved in France'. Some of the groupings were geographically logical, as demonstrated by the addition of the railways in South Wales into the GWR, others were less so. For instance, what possible connection could the Great Eastern have with the tiny GNoSR which, in any case,

The LMS with a total mainland route mileage of 7,790 was not only the largest of the four groups, but also the largest private railway system in the whole world. However, it soon became apparent that the LMS was too large and unwieldy, and commentators have since expressed the view that it would probably have been better to have merged the Midland with the Great Central. On January 1st 1922 the prelude to the formation of the LMS had been witnessed when the LNWR and the L&YR had merged to form what was then the largest railway in Britain, enjoying a route mileage of 2,667miles, employing 3,250 locomotives, which would have been bigger than the Southern on its formation in 1923. In many ways these two companies alone, possibly joined by the Furness, Maryport & Carlisle etc. would have made a sensible combination. The inclusion

of Scottish companies, in the eyes of some commentators made a complete nonsense. One of the casualties experienced north of the border was the closure of the Wanlockhead & Leadhills Light Railway on January 2nd 1939. With its closure, this ex-Caledonian branch lost the distinction of having the highest standard gauge passenger railway in Britain. The top picture shows the line near Elvanfoot prior to closure, with 0-4-2T

No.16217 leading ex-Garstang & Knott End Railway coach no.17899 and an assortment of trucks. In complete contrast, a few miles further south at Carlisle Citadel Station, LMS 4-6-2 No.6227 Duchess of Devonshire prepares to depart for Glasgow on a journey which will take it non-stop past the Elvanfoot junction station as it competes with the LNER for the prestigious Scotch traffic. BOTH AUTHOR'S COLLECTION

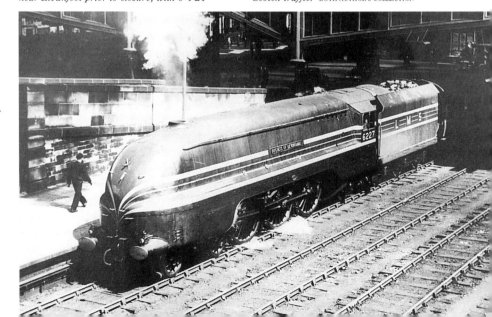

was separated from the rest of the LNER by a 38 mile stretch of what would become LMS railway between Aberdeen and Kinnaber Junction in the south. It would obviously need much fine tuning to achieve a better organised system, but the pressures were on to find an immediate solution and the most expedient way seemed to favour the amalgamation of the independent companies into four roughly geographic sections. But, how much more would we have benefited by the establishment of six separate regions with distinct boundaries, such as those evidenced after the

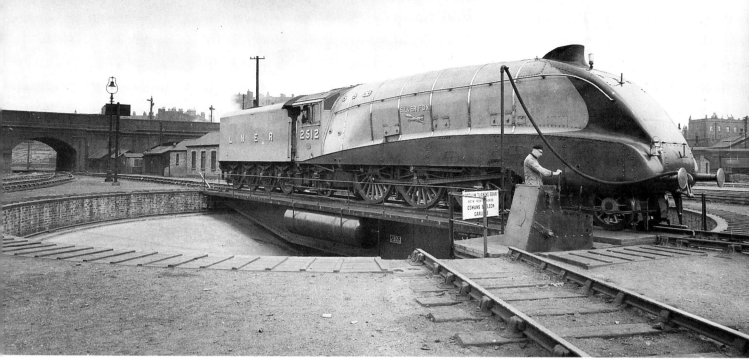

The LNER was the second largest of the four groups with a network of 6,590 route miles, and like the LMS, one of the main routes to Scotland. It was on this route where the prestige traffic was to be found more than all others. The introduction of Gresley's streamlined pacifics in September 1935 was more than revolutionary and caused, from the aesthetic view, a great deal of controversy at the time. The first four engines Silver Link, Silver King, Silver Fox, and Quicksilver with their silver/grey paint and matching coaches epitomised a new era as a Newcastle - London service, appropriately named the Silver Jubilee was inaugurated with a four hour timing for the 268 mile journey. The class were subsequently introduced on to the West Riding expresses, such as the West Riding Limited in September 1937, when Silver Fox ran the official test train completing the journey in 2hours 29minutes. Undoubtedly, the peak of the A4's prewar performance came with the attainment of 126mph at Essendine by Mallard when it gained the never to be surpassed world steam traction speed record. This undated view was probably taken in 1936, at King's Cross where No.2512 Silver Fox is being turned on the new Cowans, Sheldon turntable.

COURTESY NEI COWANS - BOYD PLC.

Nationalisation of 1948 (viz. Southern, Western, London-Midland, Eastern, North-eastern, Scottish).

The Times debated the issue in depth and its railway number of August 15th 1921 makes interesting reading, similarly an American Government publication The Re-organization of Railways In Great Britain; its progress and prospects contains numerous pages of statistics to show a comparison of probable consequences between the British situation and America's Transportation Act of 1920. These were not isolated writings, perhaps just the tip of a very large iceberg. Indeed the plethora of material which was published on railway amalgamation, nationalisation and the Grouping between 1919 and 1925 would provide several months of bed-time reading. Despite all the pronounced ideas, the Railways Act became law in August 1921 and from then onwards a number of companies began working closely together as a prelude to the Grouping. Most of the 'competing lines' schemes which had been postponed in 1914 vanished overnight, including some very logical ones which should have been continued (like the link across Bradford to join the L&YR/GNR station with

the Midland). Similarly, a large number of light railway proposals were also abandoned, as the autonomy the Light Railway Act had brought to rural parts of Britain would be adversely affected in a number of ways by the creation of four large companies. Even within the new large companies, rivalries were beginning to emerge, with questions such as who would assume the managerial positions, which works would get the new orders, which company's designs would become standard etc. all becoming important issues of the day.

Space simply does not permit us to explore these questions or the consequences of the Grouping in any depth and, anyway, other writers have already covered the subject more than admirably. It is perhaps sufficient for our purposes to recognise that major changes had taken place and more were on the way. The fact that the war brought about major changes such as the Grouping is good reason for us to record it in these pages, but when one considers that inside just six years the new companies would experience the outbreak of war again, we now need to examine how they would address the arrears of maintenance and prepare for what lay ahead.

Preparing for war again

The formation of the League of Nations in 1920 was, in the grandest of ideological dreams, the proposed means to prevent (by arbitration and conciliation) a repetition of the carnage mankind had just undergone. However, the avocation of it as 'the political expression of God's Kingdom on Earth' seemed to be taking things too far as the victors demonstrated faith in its creation by stockpiling salvaged weapons from the war which had just ended. Few Generals believed in the 'guarantee of peace' the League proffered, so they continued their own preparations for the next conflict by ordering bigger and better pieces of military hardware. The imposition of the indemnities known as reparations placed a charge of £6,600 million on Germany (plus interest) which resulted in impossible economic conditions throughout Europe. Conflict thus changed from the battlefields to banks and factories as the defeated nations were forced to make more goods to pay off their debts. In this crazy period the American banks withdrew investment from Europe, the Austrian Credit Anstalt bank collapsed and the French cancelled their short-term credits. This led to a fall in both exports and internal consumption, with a resulting drop in the need for transportation - a situation which directly affected both shipping and railways. The World Slump had arrived.

In Britain the railway companies' financial difficulties which had been experienced since the end of World War I were, in some small measure, addressed by the Development (Loan Guarantees and Grants) Act of 1929. With the

In a famous radio broadcast in 1939, a reporter on the American CBS network announced that 'the lights were going out all over Europe', and in readiness for this blackout - preparations were made by all organisations who would be effected. The railway companies effected a means of weak platform illumination by covering hurricane lamps with paper, at the front of which a small hole would be cut. Some lamps would be fitted inside with a piece of tin bent to act as a reflector, providing a more concentrated, narrow beam of light. In the build up to war several thousand such lamps were stored by the railway companies in readiness for the Air Raid Precautions. In the late summer of 1939, a London Underground Railway station is equipped with its 'illumination'.

slump continuing between 1929 and 1934, simultaneous to the growth of National Socialism in Germany, many forecast that war was again inevitable. Obviously, preparatory work had to be undertaken and as far as the railway undertakings were concerned, it was the Railways Agreement Act of 1935 which brought about most of the improvements. Whilst the finance provided through this Act only went part of the way towards helping the railway companies prepare for the coming conflict, it did enable them to begin to make a start. Traditionally, Germany's military strength had been the size of its navy and in the First World War railway traffic flows had changed to meet this threat. No longer were they exclusively supplying the south coast ports, because new anchorages and naval bases had been provided along the East Coast and up to the north of Scotland. We have already seen how new lines and connections were laid into facilitate such traffic between 1914 and 1918, but twenty years on the military and naval build up would once again have to be concentrated in the south. The reason for this lay in the

decimated state of the German Navy in 1918, and the prohibition of the construction of naval vessels over 10,000 tons imposed in the Treaty of Versailles. Unable to construct new capital ships, Germany put its energy into finding ways round the disarmament clauses of the treaty and began the creation of a magnificent air force and a large submarine fleet. The threat to Britain was obvious, so measures were taken to combat this new German menace and defensive military planning was concentrated on the south.

Because most of the existing railways to the south ran through (or radiated from) London, the railway companies had to put some serious thought into what would happen if the capital was heavily bombed and these routes were destroyed. Accordingly plans were put in hand for a new series of connections which would take the railways around the city. The Government agreed to finance these connections and associated works in order to prepare for the threat which lay ahead. Much of the preparatory work was done under auspices of the Railway Technical Committee which was

set up in 1937. In this regard, the work on improving the railways in preparation for possible conflict was, in many ways, contemporary with what was happening in British industry in general. History clearly reveals that some of the works undertaken for peace-time improvements, also had an ulterior military motive behind their conception. For example, the provision of movable gangway at Stranraer Harbour in 1938 was ostensibly to allow cars on to the deck of a steamer alongside. Yet in view of the worsening political situation it perhaps should not be surprising that the ramp was given a safe weight limit which would also allow it to carry the heaviest of tanks then employed by the British Army. A substantial Air Raid Precautions grant of £4 millions was paid to the railway companies at the end of 1938, to which the Big Four companies were expected to add a further £¾ millions from their own resources. This money was spent not only on air raid precautions such as shelters, fire-fighting equipment and so on, but also to ensure that the staff could cope with any problems which might be caused through precision enemy bombing of the railways.

A significant preparatory programme carried out early in 1939 saw the construction of a number of 'evacuation trains', designed for use after heavy air raids on cities when city hospitals may not be able to cope. These trains were to have nine bogie vans for the conveyance of stretchers and a further three coaches to provide support facilities. The bulk of the vehicles used for stretcher cases were GWR 'Siphon G' bogie vans, but fitted with corridor connections and steam heating. As these vans would be needed in daily service until such time as hostilities were commenced, they were returned to service after conversion, the stretcher brackets being fastened on the under-frames ready for fitting when the need arose. When the Railway Executive eventually

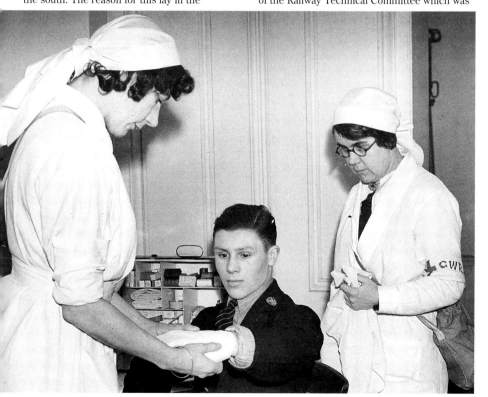

First aid training was a significant part of war preparations, not least of which was the expansion of the Railway Ambulance classes held by different companies. In a number of larger stations special casualty 'stations' were prepared in readiness to handle emergency situations. One such facility was the Royal Waiting Room at Paddington station, which was so equipped after the valuable pieces of 'period' furniture were removed and taken into store. In this view a youthful GWR employees receive the ministrations of two GWR nurses.
ATLANTIC COLLECTION

called them into service, the GWR were able to locate the vehicles and complete the work, then deliver the trains inside just three days. In January 1939 a massive blackout exercise was held on the railways, with the most significant test being conducted on the GWR between Paddington and Old Oak Common. A train was converted to the Home Office screened lighting standards, but the tests demonstrated that these standards were far to low to allow railway operations to be carried out in safety.

At the outbreak of war, the railways had been brought up to generally good condition, considering the state in which they emerged from World War I. There were over 37,000 miles of running lines, which had seen the vast sum of £315,500,000 spent on their development in the preceding decade. The best train services were the most modern in the world, and only the year before *Mallard* had

Above: *Some military training was provided, as it was considered essential that members of the certain branches of the forces should become familiar with railway operation. In many previous conflicts, this lack of understanding of railway matters by the military had caused more disruption to train services than had been occasioned by enemy action. During the American Civil War, the assistant Secretary of War wrote to the commander of the Military Railroad in Virginia, advising 'Be patient as possible with the Generals. Some of them will trouble you more than the enemy'. By World War II, Britain had its military and railway liaisons well organised, and where possible the railway companies did all they could to accommodate the armed forces. One example is this LNER locomotive instruction coach pictured here in 1941, where members of the forces were being trained as railwaymen.*
LNER OFFICIAL PICTURE, COURTESY DAVID JENKINSON

Below: *On a Ministry directive, the Forestry Commission began the production of timber for 'railway purposes', with dimensions which would indicate this being used for sleepers, bridge timber, shoring work and shuttering. These supplies were allocated to strategic points around the country, placed in readiness for a possible bombing campaign on the railways. The railways were also allowed to purchase equipment to effect these repairs; for example the LMS ordered two batches of light-weight permanent way cranes from Cowans, Sheldon in Carlisle. Mounted on a well-wagon, 15 of these highly useful cranes were rated at 6´ ton and five were 10 tons. One of these is pictured in the St. Nicholas Works prior to delivery in 1940.*
NEI COWANS - BOYD PLC

COWANS SHELDON
CARLISLE.

Above, left: *As pictured on pages 76-82, the railways took air raid precautions very seriously. Not only did it encourage competitions in ambulance work, but also in fire-fighting. The railways held an annual competition, with the finals taking place at Marylebone Goods Yard. Jetting his way into the finals, a representative of the GWR from South Wales works his way forward with his hose, helmet and axe.*

ATLANTIC COLLECTION

Above, right: *Another preparation for war was the decision to obliterate nameboards and other signs which might be useful in giving directions to the enemy. Although it was primarily designed to confuse parachutists, it was also suggested that 'station name signs and other such nameboards, might provide enemy airmen with navigational aids.' Whilst this might have been true of the few Southern stations which had their names painted on the roofs (for the benefit of people flying from Croydon to France), the others could hardly have given much succour to Luftwaffe navigators. Nevertheless, the orders stood, and station signs like this at Esher were duly obliterated.*

NATIONAL RAILWAY MUSEUM

taken the world speed record for a steam powered locomotive. Not only the LNER, but on the Southern, Great Western and LMS too, many express locomotives and much of the associated coaching stock had been built to the most modern designs. If Britain's politicians or army was not fully equipped for the outbreak of war, its railways were. Yet before considering how the railways were operated during the war years, we must first consider the basis on which compensation for war service would be paid. As in World War I, with the outbreak of war, the Emergency Powers (Defence) Act would be invoked, whereby the Government would take control of the railways and vest power into a Railway Executive Committee which would be formed of railway company officers who were to act as agents of the Crown. Preliminary talks in 1937 had debated the issue of payment for war service, no doubt the lack of adequate compensation being paid to the railway companies after 1918 being very much at the back of everyone's mind. The 1921 Railways Act had set a 'standard revenue' for the railway

companies, and it was expected that this would be the basis for compensation to the various railway Boards. However, because the standard revenue had never been earned in peace time (due to external circumstances like the slump), the Government proposed compensation should be based on the agregate earnings of the railways over the three years prior to the war. In the end this was amended to the average earned in the years 1935-7. The railway companies objected however, because they could see that the rates were far too low to adequately compensate for the traffic that would have to be carried in times of war. Indeed, it later transpired that a far greater burden was thrown upon the railways than was ever envisaged; so great was the expansion of traffic that it caused a much more intensive use of capital assets employed. Furthermore, in setting maintenance and renewal figures at the 1935-7 levels, it would be impossible to prevent a massive backlog of such work from building up. In entering the war under these terms, the railway companies were already sowing the

Road versus rail

By contrast with what existed a quarter of a century earlier, the roads in Britain had improved immeasurably by 1939. Two factors were significant in this accomplishment, both of which were connected with the ending of the Great War. Firstly, the declaration of peace had resulted in large disposals of military equipment including a massive number of ex-War Department and U.S. Army lorries which then brought a minor revolution in road-haulage. Acquired by a wide variety of new owners, these solid-wheel Fords, Leylands, Peerless and Thorneycrofts etc. did not individually offer substantial competition to the railways but they were a cumulative threat nevertheless. Coupled with this, a gradual improvement of roads came about in the 1920s as the second factor in our equation, the Depression, took hold. The railway companies, suffering badly from the loss of traffic and new competition, were quick to address the threat to its small load - single destination business, recognising that many of the new owner-drivers would undercut them to a point of negligible profitability just to get the trade and thereby keep alive. For example, the Southern and LNER noticed a significant drop in continental traffic to the channel ports, Harwich etc.

All the major railways invested heavily in new road delivery systems, particularly the GWR and LMS. The creation of a country lorry service secured some, but by no means all, of the traffic

that was flowing away from the railways. But it was not until the Road & Rail Traffic Act of 1933, that a licensing system was introduced to regulate and restrict entry into the road haulage business. The brave new era of road transportation was also seeing an increase in 'out of town' bus services, with a number of firms making significant inroads into traffic which had previously been the exclusive preserve of the railways. For instance, the LNER found that one of its East Anglian competitors, United Automobile Services, had spread into the North-east where the NER had once enjoyed a virtual monopoly. However, from 1928 onwards the railways began using new powers to object to the licensing of bus services where it could be proved that there was unused railway capacity. More positively, the railways began buying into bus company holdings, significantly in areas where they could see that improved road services would erode their position.

In looking through lorry and bus adverts for 1939, one cannot fail to be impressed by the standards manufacturers had reached inside two decades - the threat to the railways was very real. However, at the same time there was still a very poor long distance network, many roads still being winding legacies of the days of horse and cart. So, when Chamberlain declared war in 1939, once again the only means of rapid transport that existed to move men, munitions and machinery were Britain's railways - the story of what happened in the next five and a half years is an absorbing one.

Above: *Although the LMS was making considerable progress towards converting its road-haulage fleet over to motor vehicle operation, at the outset of the war it still had a very large number of horse drawn vehicles. For a variety of reasons, the Grouped companies adapted very slowly to change, when its competitors were rapidly seizing the opportunities provided in war surplus vehicles. However, as early as 1919, the L&YR had secured a fleet of ex-American Army lorries, and sent these to depots (such as Holmfirth in West Yorkshire) where it was experiencing trouble from haulage sub-contractors who were continually increasing their prices. Unfortunately the LMS did not rapidly expand upon this formula after the grouping, so that by 1939 heavy horses such as this one pictured here with Miss Vera Proctor were still at work in cities like Bristol.*
ATLANTIC COLLECTION

Left: *On the other hand, a number of firms were seeing the benefits which could be obtained by instituting local motor-lorry collections/deliveries and tying these in with the national railway network. One such example was the Express Dairy at Appleby in Westmorland, where this Leyland lorry is unloading eggs collected from local farms at the packing station. Once cleaned and graded, these eggs would be on the way to London, travelling in an express rated goods van at the back of a passenger working or behind one of the trains of glass-lined, 6-wheeled milk tankers that were dispatched daily from the dairy's private siding on the Settle- Carlisle line.*
AUTHORS COLLECTION

1939 -1945

What the railways had prepared for! *The Southern's ARP programme was put to dramatic test on the night of August 13th 1940 when Portsmouth Harbour was blitzed.*

Introduction To World War Two

By the early summer of 1939 it seemed as though a World War was once again inevitable, despite the placatory efforts of politicians like Neville Chamberlain to avert a conflict with Germany. As late as August that year Hitler was saying that 'Germany has never sought conflict with England....she has, for years, endeavoured to win England's friendship.' Few were convinced by this, the League of Nations had proved to be an abysmal failure and the world lived in terror, but few had any real idea of what this war would bring. Early in 1939, the famous author and military aircraft designer, Nevil Shute published a book of fiction about the sort of circumstances which might be experienced at the outbreak of hostilities. In *What Happened To The Corbetts* he presented an account of the destruction that mass bombing would bring to a town like Southampton. The book was widely criticised on publication by civic and Government officials alike, but Shute did not care about the reaction. Writing to the public through the press he said: 'if I have held your attention for an evening, if I have given to the least of your officials one new idea to ponder and digest, then I feel that my book will have played a part in preparing us for the terrible things that you, and I, and all the citizens of the cities in this country, may one day have to face'.

Shute's semi-prophetic book might have caused an uproar in early 1939, but today it presents a fascinating picture of the conceptions held by ordinary people in the last few months before war. The mass bombing described by Shute did not come in 1939, indeed a further year was to elapse before the concentrated efforts of the Luftwaffe were experienced by the citizens of all the cities in this country. At first a 'phoney war' was experienced, with British and German aircraft dumping propaganda leaflets from their bomb bays instead of high-explosive. Lord Haw Haw, the propaganda voice of Germany, boomed out across the air waves thanking the British for their contribution to the German War Effort - the leaflets dropped by the RAF were being collected and recycled into toilet paper!

The British war in Europe began with the mobilisation of the British Expeditionary Force, who were promptly embarked for France and the Low Countries. However, even at the time of their embarkation, the Ministry of War recognised that whatever the outcome of the battles on the Continent, there was no prospect

Though horse-power was generally out-dated in WW2, it was still used in some theatres of war. Here mules for a mountain battery are loaded at the ex-LNWR station at Weedon on April 22nd 1940. The station saw a considerable amount of horse traffic due to its proximity to an Army Equestrian Centre.

of bringing the bulk of the BEF's mechanised equipment back home. Accordingly, much of the equipment was sent overseas with demolition devices or instructions devised to prevent it falling into enemy hands. Meanwhile, on the continent, the reliance which the non-axis nations had put into static defence systems etc was soon demonstrated to be out-dated; German strategy had obviously progressed far beyond the attritious forms of warfare which had resulted in the defeat of the Kaiser's forces in 1918. Trenches and fortified emplacements were no match for a highly mechanised fighting force, but the real success lay in the issue of aerial superiority. In Poland the world witnessed the effects of Blitzkrieg (lightening war) as the German airborne forces swept over the static defences. On the ground, Polish cavalry troops proved no match against the mighty Panzer tanks.

In April 1940 the British witnessed the superiority of the new German warfare in Norway, when it was demonstrated that naval power could no longer be relied upon as a deterrent in areas where the enemy held command of the air. By the second week of May the Nazis had swarmed into the Low Countries, where it was soon clear that the Allies were utterly outclassed. As the invaders swept round the northern side of the Maginot line, it became apparent that the great French fortification built between 1929-34 was completely useless. In just a few short weeks the German war machine had by-passed the defended frontier from Luxembourg to Switzerland and punched a hole through the unprotected Franco-Belgian border. By the end of May the BEF had fallen back on Dunkirk, from where a flotilla of small craft repatriated the exhausted and demoralised soldiers back to Britain. French resistance

Just a few weeks before Dunkirk, troops leave for France. Chalked messages on the carriage sides being typical of the farewell scenes on stations around the country. KEYSTONE LIBRARY

crumbled and an armistice was signed with Germany on June 20th. Even though the last of the Maginot forts did not surrender until ten days later, the line was captured intact, except for a few outlying defences at Saarbrücken. France fell and the Vichy Government was installed on July 10th - for Hitler there came the added bonus of the capture of the French west coast ports, allowing easy access for the German U-Boat fleet into the North Atlantic. This was now the prelude for the start of the next German offensive, which began with the Battle of Britain and Hitler's desire to eliminate all the air bases in the south of England as a preparation for invasion. By 1941, the German army were poised on the shores of France, looking longingly towards their next conquest on the opposite side of La Manche. So, nearly nine centuries after the last successful invasion of Britain by the Normans in 1066, the island fortress stood alone.

Resolutely against the might of Hitler's Luftwaffe, the RAF won the Battle of Britain and brought valuable breathing space to a beleaguered nation. Unable to defeat the single seat fighter squadrons (formed from aircraft like the Spitfire and Hurricane), in the autumn of 1940 Hitler ordered a change of tactics. This in turn, saw the commencement of the mass bombing tactics foretold by aviation experts like Shute. This was the beginning of the blitz, through which the nation would be tested to the limit of endurance. There was an almost pathological fear of gas attack but this failed to materialise though high-explosive and incendiary devices rained down on almost every city and industrial conurbation throughout the realm. To protect the civilian population enormous measures were introduced, including the major Air Raid Precaution programme which had been started in the prewar era. Part of the ARP began in September 1939 with the evacuation of vulnerable members of the community from major cities, moving large numbers to comparative safety in the country or by the seaside. In addition the pitiful sights of children being transported to a new life away from their parents, the railway stations of Britain began to take on a dramatic change of appearance. Under the control of the Railway Executive Committee again, the rail system swung once more towards a nationally coordinated programme that same month. The Big Four, London Transport and a few minor railways were all charged with the task of moving men and supplies essential for the country's independence.

As the tide of war changed, so did the role of the railways which saw the first signs of the offensive with the embarkation of the 1st Army for North Africa in 1942. This was followed by the movement of forces coming to this country from the Commonwealth nations and (later) the USA, prior to the opening of a second front. Supplies were transported to ports and air-bases around the country, with large volumes of equipment going to what has often been described as Britain's forgotten army, the servicemen who took on the might of the Imperial Japanese Army in India, Burma and the Far East. By early 1944 the preparations were well underway for the invasion of France, which would be later known as D-Day. Between November 1943 and October 1944, the weight of traffic carried in connection with the build up to, and following, the Normandy landings is probably incalculable. But throughout, the railways took the strain as men and equipment had the very last ounce of energy squeezed out of them. After VE day the railways began the repatriation of the fighting men who had survived the hostilities, re-uniting them with their families; but sadly many thousands who had said goodbye to their loved ones on a crowded platform station, never did return.

The pages which follow are but a brief glimpse of those troubled times between 1939 and 1945, in which we try to portray almost every aspect of life on the working railways of Britain during the war years. The sections cover air raid and anti-gas precautions, bombing, underground tube shelters and the evacuation of children. How the railways were kept running (albeit frequently late running), is shown in context with the exceptional increase in freight and armament traffic. A unique view is also afforded of the lesser known side of railway operations in the war, including catering, luggage, hospital trains, and the large scale use of women employees. We also look in on the work of the railway workshops, which not only supplied locomotives and rolling stock for use at home and abroad, but produced a large quantity of other essential war equipment as well. Finally, this part of the story is concluded with sections on armoured trains, accidents and disasters. However, it should be stressed that each section is not just a collection of train pictures, but rather a look at how railways played a vital role in the social history of the period between 1939 and 1945.

Air raid precautions

The vast railway marshalling yards, key junctions and major stations became places of strategic importance and thus susceptible to enemy attack. During World War I, a number of raids were made on Britain's railway installations by the German Zeppelin airships. With more modern aircraft at its disposal, the Luftwaffe had ample capacity to inflict severe damage upon the railways, as had been evidenced in Poland, France and the Low Countries at the start of the war.

Air raid precautions were at first quite simple, involving a general blackout and the provision of fire buckets. The real threat was considered to be gas, and all railway crews were issued with gas masks. They were also amongst the first civilians provided with steel helmets, to offer protection from flying shrapnel.

Signalmen were given small steel cabinets in which they could enclose

Above: *To combat fire at railway installations, the GWR formed three mobile fire-fighting trains. Crewed by eight men, they were manned 24 hours a day, sleeping and eating accommodation being provided on the train.*

Left: *By February 28th 1941 the railway 'fire-men' had become totally proficient, but still continued to practise; as is shown in this view with crews unloading trailer-pumps from a Covered Carriage Truck (CCT) using block and tackle.*

Opposite: *To offer protection to its footplate crews, the Southern Railway had issued them all with steel helmets by September 18th 1939.*

themselves during an air raid. These were found to be necessary after a signalman was killed by flying glass in his box in the Midlands. Being behind a large body of glass, he had been killed by the blast of a bomb a quarter of a mile away; but more seriously his death resulted in an accident to a train under his control. Although only two passengers were actually hurt in the derailment, it resulted in a blockage of a major junction which took two days to clear with all the attendant delays to traffic. Generally the shelters were not liked, and most signalmen resorted to them only when bombs were falling in the immediate vicinity.

Fire alarms and air-raid warning gongs were established in railway yards, where the civilian sirens were not easily heard due to the background noise. These alarms were usually under the care of the yard foreman or the station master, and only on his instructions could they be sounded. At some establishments it was common to sound the alarm much later than the civilian siren, in order to keep the men working right up to the last possible moment before an attack. During the hours of darkness, look-outs were stationed in the railway yards, often on signal gantries or up yard lamps, from where they could have a commanding view of the establishment they were protecting – watching out for attacking aircraft or fires which might be started. In all, 170,000 railwaymen and women received ARP training in the first four years of war.

Fire-fighting was yet another specialised task that was also taught to railwaymen; in all, 73 special fire-fighting trains were constructed and stationed at key points outside major towns and cities, to be brought into use in any case of emergency. On the Southern Railway, orders were given for several of these trains to be made up; these were to comprise six old locomotive tenders specially converted as water carriers, a coach providing sleeping and living accommodation for eight men, a covered carriage truck (CCT) holding the pumps, and a stores van carrying auxiliary fire-fighting equipment. Similarly the GWR developed its own fire-fighting trains, but preferred to concentrate on road trailer pumps, capable of delivering 150 gallons

On no account must this gong be sounded other than for air raid warning.

of water per minute. However the off-loading of these vehicles away from stations proved to be both difficult and time consuming, until block and tackle equipment was fitted to the vans for use where no platform existed.

In many goods yards, and alongside other major railway centres, emergency dams were constructed as static water points, most with a capacity of around 100,000 gallons. Special hydrants were constructed to take supplies from locomotive watering facilities such as water cranes, parachute tanks and tank houses. Everywhere, it became common practice to distribute large numbers of sand-buckets, whilst shunting engines and guards vans were equipped with hose-pipes and stirrup pumps to enable crews to deal with fires where the brigade engines couldn't reach.

Left: *King's Cross shed on the LNER was one of the company's most important depots. Consequently very serious measures were taken to protect both it and its staff from air attack. High-pitched metallic gongs are seen being erected on November 26th 1939, after it was found that ordinary alarms could not be heard over the noise of locomotives. Also of interest are the hand-bell and rattle contained in the cabinet below. The practice of painting white lines on the corners of buildings became common after the introduction of the black-out.*

Top Right: *Following the signal box tragedy in the Midlands, the LMS issued a tall steel cabinet to many of their boxes. This Air Raid Precaution (ARP) cabinet was designed to offer protection from flying shards of glass during bombing raids; however they became irreverently known as 'tin coffins' and many were used for little more than storage lockers.*

Bottom Right: *In 1937 the LMS combined secretly with the Home Office to build a special ARP train at the Wolverton Works. It first appeared in the autumn containing two coaches equipped with de-contaminating equipment, and coaches fitted out as ARP training centres. It became known as the 'yellow train' and is seen here at Euston with the guard wearing a gas mask and special gloves.*

The major precaution was of course the blackout, and some extraordinary lengths were taken to ensure the blackout was maintained. In some cases coach windows were completely painted out, whilst in others a narrow strip was painted down the sides covering the gap on either side of the blind. Low watt or blue bulbs were placed in coach compartment lights, and lineside braziers and fog 'devils' were encapsulated in metal containers; but despite all precautions, some trains were still easily spotted at night. My grandparents' house was almost a mile away from the ex-LNWR Standedge line, yet I am told that the glow from the chimneys could quite easily be identified as locomotives laboured toward the summit. It was perhaps inevitable that no blackout could be totally enforced where live steam was concerned, but all in all

Left: *Roof spotting and fire watching became an important part of home defence, and despite the fact that it involved sitting in a lonely exposed position in all weathers, hundreds of men did their bit every night of the year. As he climbs to his 'Jim Crow' nest at Camden Shed on November 29th 1940, this LMS spotter has a commanding view of Royal Scot 4-6-0 No 6119* Lancashire Fusilier, *with Chalk Farm Station to the rear.*

Opposite Top: *The all important black-out was rigorously enforced, particularly on the railways. Low watt bulbs were placed in carriage lights, and shades then placed around them. On top of this, the windows were often painted black, as is shown in this view taken at Ashford in September 1939.*

Opposite Bottom: *Where entire carriage windows were to be blacked-out it wasn't sufficient to paint just a single side, as this could become abraded in the course of normal daily use – letting light through as a result. Accordingly, both inside and outside were painted, as is evidenced at the Derby carriage works, where these withdrawn dining cars are receiving attention. This black-out was applied a month after the outbreak of war, when the dining cars had been withdrawn. However, they were re-introduced on October 12th 1939, and this work shows the preparation for that return to service.*

the railways made a determined effort to conceal themselves.

Unfortunately a number of lives were lost in Britain's railway yards and engine sheds during the war, not by enemy attack, but by the measures taken to prevent them. Railway installations are notoriously dangerous places even in daylight, becoming even worse in the hours of darkness with just dim lighting being provided for safety reasons. However all such lighting was extinguished during the war, and consequently hazards abounded to trap the unfamiliar or the unwary. A number of deaths are recorded where railwaymen (and women) fell into obstacles like ash pits, turntable wells, and inspection pits. Other instances relate of workers being run over or crushed during shunting operations in the goods yards. To help prevent such accidents corners of buildings and the edge of pits were painted white which aided visibility. In one region there was an experiment with painting wagon buffers white, though due to the nature of their use were found to be in constant need of re-painting and the idea was abandoned.

Allied to air raid precautions were the efforts made to guard key railway centres,

Below: A copy of the Air Raid Precaution notices which were pasted in the carriages, as seen on the coach window pictured above.

ARP(R)

AIR RAID PRECAUTIONS
INSTRUCTIONS TO PASSENGERS

If an air raid occurs while you are in the train:

1. Do NOT attempt to leave the train if it stops AWAY FROM A STATION unless requested by the guard to do so. You are safer where you are.

2. Pull the blinds down both by day and night, as a protection against flying glass.

3. If room is available lie down on the floor.

junctions and tunnels where, at the outbreak of the war, regular soldiers or reservists appeared on sentry duty. In due course these men were moved elsewhere, as more detachments of local defence volunteers were established. These units eventually became known as the Home Guard and railway employees played an important role in the movement, with around 90,000 workers becoming part-time soldiers. If this number is added to the 170,000 employed in ARP duties, it comes to a staggering total of 260,000 or about half the total workforce. During the course of their daily work, railwaymen were often called upon to face additional perils, particularly while handling live ammunition. In all these activities the railwaymen exhibited acts of devotion, and in a number of cases went much further and showed courage above and beyond the call of duty. Not only were these acts of courage recognised by the railway companies, but in many instances medals were awarded including the George Cross, the George Medal, and the British Empire Medal.

Bomb damage

Despite all the precautions, the inevitable still happened, and the railway network suffered some quite major damage. All over the British Isles, railway installations were affected. The later tactics of 'train-busting' employed by RAF and USAF fighter pilots using Hurricane, Mustang and Kittihawk aircraft was not successfully copied by the Luftwaffe except for occasional and seemingly haphazard attacks in the southern counties. Therefore the opportunity of semi-paralysing the nation through systematic concentration on its railways, was one which the German High Command apparently overlooked. Yet Britain, stretched as it was in the early years of the war, had become highly dependent on its railway network; had the latter been systematically attacked, then conceivably a German invasion might have succeeded.

In fact Britain had one major asset; a multitude of routes, its legacy from the pre-grouping days. This plethora of alternatives gave the Railway Executive a variety of options for re-routing trains away from damage affected areas. Therefore, lines which had almost been a virtual liability in the pre-war years were now proving to be of vital strategic

Top: *In the course of World War II, over 12,000 tons of high explosive was dropped on London, six times more than any other provincial city. Almost half the country's 60,595 civilian dead were killed in the London region, with many more injured. Damage to railway installations was therefore inevitable, as exemplified by this view of the damage caused at Liverpool Street on the night of September 8th 1940.*

Bottom: *It was not only static targets that were at danger, as is portrayed by this view near Ingatestone. The train was travelling between Shenfield and Ingatestone when the track in front of it received a direct hit. As the train was travelling at the compulsory 20mph speed limit during air raids, there were no fatalities or serious injury. Considerable damage was caused to both locomotive and stock when it fell into the resulting bomb crater.*

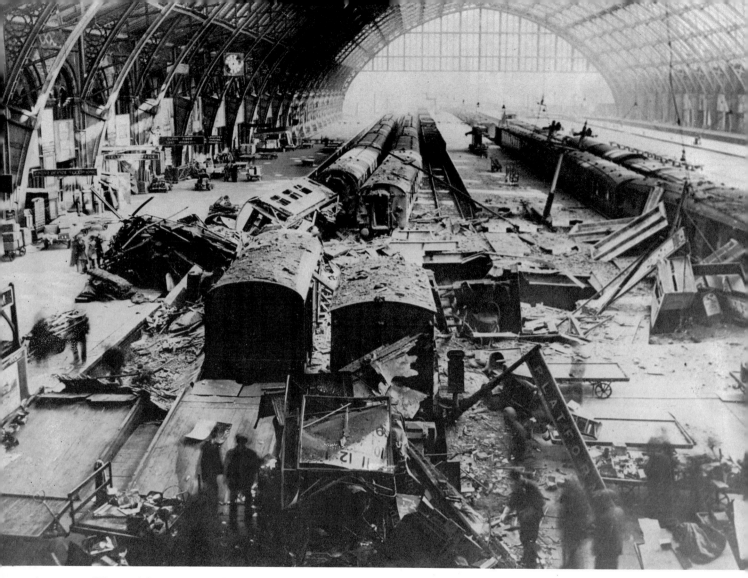

importance. When aerial attack occurred, whether by incendiary devices, land mines or bombs, the various regional committees of the Executive usually had a variety of choices at their disposal, and could often re-route trains without causing major delays.

Even so, damage frequently occurred where no alternative routes were possible, particularly in large city terminal stations, where the Executive had to effect speedy repairs. A rapid repair organisation was established in the early months of the war and within a short period had become so efficient that it could achieve amazing results. Main line tracks were repaired and restored to full running in a few hours, whilst bridges could be replaced within a day. To achieve this, permanent breakdown crews were put on stand-by at key centres, whilst prefabricated bridge spans, signal-box kits, and other repair materials were located at important junctions on the

Above: *In a daylight raid on 10th May 1941, the damage to St Pancras Station looks pretty serious. Despite the apparent devastation, trains were running again inside 9 hours.*

outskirts of towns and cities. When an attack resulted in damage, the repair teams swung into action, the work often commencing before the 'all-clear' was sounded. Even so, some major tasks had to be left as they were, or in a patched up condition until well after the war.

In a daylight raid on a London station, the surface platforms, and the connecting underground station were badly damaged; despite the apparent devastation, trains were again running through inside nine hours. The following day, a repaired station, complete with a new booking office was re-opened. Elsewhere in the city a vitally important station was so badly damaged, that an electric train had been blown off its track onto the platforms. All the running lines in and out of the station were either destroyed or blocked, but within 24 hours normal service had been resumed.

Damage was not limited to the major cities like London, Birmingham and Glasgow; small towns like Whitby also suffered, as did village stations and isolated sections of railway, hit by sneak German 'tip and run' raids. However, whether it was in a large city or in a rural location, the railways were quickly repaired – all part of the great effort to keep the nation's vital communications open.

Below: *One week later, the scene has been transformed. LMS railway engineers have repaired the damaged platforms, the famous single span roof remains almost undamaged. For security reasons, neither of these pictures were released to the press until 26th August 1942.*

Evacuees

The most moving sights on railway stations during World War II were the pitiful groups of children, lonely and bemused, walking around with little cardboard labels identifying both them and their luggage as evacuees. The consequences of a mass evacuation with heart-rending scenes of parting and fretful children in railway stations, may well be looked on as just one of the sad faces of a country at war. However, in social terms it could be said that the whole evacuation programme was an unmitigated disaster.

The Government had anticipated that bombs would begin falling as soon as war was declared, and consequently began the evacuation of children, pregnant women and the elderly on Friday September 1st 1939. All the stations of the great cities were swamped with thousands of people, who had been advised to seek refuge in the countryside or smaller towns. The fact that bombs did not fall was no fault of the Government, but the problems caused by the extreme measures it had taken fell upon the railways to sort out.

An estimated 3,500,000 evacuees were expected, but barely a third of that number arrived at the stations. Those that did arrive came in vast surges, usually early in the day congesting the platforms and waiting rooms. This threw the railway organisation into disarray, with all the carefully co-ordinated plans going out of the window. As there was no Government organisation to clear up the mess, it was left to station officials to clear the crowds the best way they could. In a large number of cases this was accomplished by loading people on to the first train to come into the station, regardless of either it or its passengers' actual destination.

In terms of a railway operation it worked well, with over 800,000 children alone being moved in three days, without anyone getting killed, injured or even lost. In social terms it was a disaster, with bewildered station-masters and billeting officers sorting out the chaos at the other end. Stations where 300 children were expected would receive but a few dozen, whilst those with no plans for evacuees could receive up to 500, who in turn became dependent on the good will of local people for a bed for the night.

Another problem was experienced in the type of some of the stock employed, with children (who frequently need the toilet) often being packed into non-corridor trains. This was exacerbated by the fact that journeys which usually took an hour could take anything up to five times longer. For example one train from London to Somerset was forced to terminate in Berkshire when the plaintive cries of the young passengers could be ignored no longer.

Evacuee traffic continued through the war, with many unable to settle away

from the big cities returning home after a few days, then fleeing again when prolonged periods of enemy attack began. Added to this, there were the occasional return trips home for holidays, funerals, and family gatherings; in short, a tide of human flotsam ebbing and flowing between city life and safety throughout the dark days of war.

Opposite: *If every boy's dream was to become an engine driver, then those pictured on this unidentified LNER class A4 Pacific in 1939 must have had the thrill of a lifetime. The compassion of railway employees for the evacuees was frequently in evidence as railwaymen showed their precious charges to children facing an uncertain future.*

Below: *Children evacuated from the big cities were not away from home all the time and at certain times of the year were re-united with their families. This Christmas scene at Waterloo Station in 1944 was therefore a familiar one to travellers of the day.*

Right: *With the collapse of France in 1940, the coastal areas of South-East England were no longer considered to be safe for the refugees from London. Some 48,000 children had to be uprooted once more, and were transported away by 70 trains which headed for destinations on the GWR and LMS. Once more this traumatic upheaval was eased by railway staff, as is shown in this view at an unidentified Southern Railway station.*

The threat of gas

It may seen strange to relate that the all consuming fear in the early days of the war was the threat of gas attack. This pathological fear stemmed, not from some alarmist official, but from evidence existing in every town, city and village. Almost everyone knew about someone who had been killed, or disabled by the gas attacks employed by the Germans in World War I. Mustard gas was one of the most terrible, which left survivors blind or with damaged lungs; so twenty years on from the armistice, horrible reminders of this abhorrent form of warfare abounded.

The first anti-gas tactics were formulated long before the start of the war, a result of the Air Raid Precautions Department training programme which commenced in 1935. By January 1937, the first civilian gas masks became available, though these offered little comfort to women with elaborate hair-styles and make up, nor to men with beards. On the

Above: *The anti-gas and decontamination trains introduced by the GWR, were kept at constant readiness throughout the war with crews adhering to fixed training schedules. The mustard coloured coaches are shown here with crews practising connecting hoses to fill water tanks, essential for the operation of the hot and cold showers in the decontamination coach.*

Right: *Meanwhile on the LNER, ARP and anti-gas training was given to employees in all avenues of the railway service. This particular instruction is provided in a converted first class Gresley LNER dining car. The coach entered service on August 17th 1938, and is seen at King's Cross station during the first lecture.*

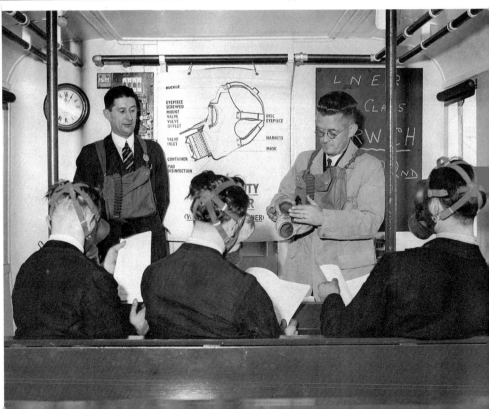

other hand, many children relished wearing them, thanks to being told that it made them look like 'Mickey Mouse'.

The grim necessity of anti-gas measures was impressed on all railway employees, and a fine was imposed by one division on the LMS from November 1937 for men failing to carry a gas mask when they signed on for duty. Whether or not this practice became universal, is not known, but by 1938 training began in earnest. At first railwaymen training in ARP duties were exposed to the smell of mustard, musty hay, pear-drops and geraniums. This was followed by exposure to tear-gas in a sealed room, and finally by giving them small whiffs of the actual gasses.

To further combat the danger, the railways formulated a much stronger strategy for dealing with gas attack by introducing special decontamination and de-gassing trains. Some 47 special cleansing vans were converted to provide facilities for areas where no decontamination equipment existed, or where existing arrangements were inadequate. Each van was provided with an air-lock, leading to a zinc lined shower-room, a third section was provided as a dressing room with fresh clothing. In addition to normal blackout, the vans were also provided with blast-proof windows.

It was considered that even though the Germans had not used gas in their earlier attacks, it was extremely likely that it would be employed at some later stage. Indeed, in several attacks in 1944 some of the V bomb warheads contained gas as opposed to high-explosives. Though this was purely a means to demoralise the civilian population, and the gas was quite ineffective and dissipated quite quickly, the threat was taken seriously and anti-gas measures were retained until the final days of the war. Even as late as January 1945 details of training in such precautions continued to be recorded by the railway companies.

Right: *Even at a late stage in the war, the threat of gas was still paramount and railway employees were impressed into the reality of working under gas-attack situations. In September 1943 a Southern Railway breakdown gang, looking more like deep sea divers, exercise somewhere in Kent.*

In the tube

The most vivid pictures of the London blitz are those of the deep underground shelters afforded by the railway system of the London Passenger Transport Board – the tube. At this point of time it might seem incredible to relate that at first the government tried to discourage their use, fearing the development of a 'shelter mind', with a population burrowing ever deeper to escape the rain of bombs. This attitude was overcome by people buying the cheapest possible ticket, officially entering as passengers, but in reality becoming shelterers. Eventually the Government was forced to succumb to popular pressure, and in all seventy-nine tube stations were provided as shelter for between 75,000 and 100,000 Londoners.

In fact several tube stations (particularly the older ones) were not very safe as they were located just below street level. At Balham one bomb actually penetrated the station where around 600 had sought refuge. Many were killed outright, with even more being drowned when a water main shattered. Water was in fact a major concern for LPTB engineers, who feared flooding of the system, by the Thames. To overcome this problem a series of floodgates were constructed at strategic points around the system, allowing the facility to seal off sections of the system in case the river broke through.

At certain stations bunks were available by reservation, as were floor spaces, but generally it was on a first come – first served basis. As a consequence, a pattern soon emerged which lasted until the last V2 'Flying Bomb' landed on London in 1945. Usually an older child would arrive first, around

school closing time, and armed with bedding and the like would proceed to stake out their family's space. The first choice were the platforms at the deeper levels, and inevitably this created congestion in the latter part of the day. To ensure free running of trains, and access for the true passengers, LPTB insisted in painting a white line 8ft from the platform

edge. In this space, no bedding or baggage could be put down until after 7.30pm, after this the distance between sleeping area and platform edge was reduced to 4ft.

Despite all the camaraderie, the sing-songs, and the community spirit, the tube shelters were not the most glamorous of places. Once the 'all-clear' was sounded people left as quickly as they could,

leaving behind huge piles of rubbish, including human and animal excretia. A few bombed-out families made semi-permanent homes in the 'dead-end' stations on the Liverpool St extension, however, the vast majority were glad to quickly escape from the dirty, draughty, lice-infested shelters.

Opposite Right: *Life in the tube was one of the great social levellers of all time, with the middle and working classes coming into intimate contact. They were not the cleanest of places, but the squalor and dirt below ground was much to be preferred to Herr Hitler's bombs above. This view in Aldwych Station with the bowler hat, the head scarf, and paper headlines says it all.*

Opposite Left: *Aldwych was a shelter where concerts were provided to while away the long evenings. It was rather untypical in that during the war, services to the station had been withdrawn, so the track area could also be used for a variety of activities like concerts and shows which were provided by theatre companies, and organisations like ENSA. To provide a stage, the platform was used, and the audience sat on the trackbed – naturally the current had been disconnected!*

Top Right: *Each afternoon six 'Tube Refreshment Specials' left individual depots, like this 4-car pre-1938 set at Cockfosters Depot on December 12th 1940. They carried around seven tons of food and refreshments, and it is significant that the train pictured here is on the line adjacent to the doorway leading to the depot canteen. The specials ran on the Bakerloo, Central, Northern and Piccadilly lines and supplied 134 canteens which served the 79 tube (and one Southern Railway) underground shelters. Every night 1,000 women worked on the service which was run on a non-profitmaking basis. Services began in 1940 and ran until 1942, but were resumed in 1943 after the commencement of the flying bomb attacks.*

Right: *On September 11th 1939, the LPTB announced the immediate closure of the Northern line between Kennington and Strand, and between Moorgate and London Bridge. This involved closing 19 stations, whilst engineers installed a series of floodgates to protect the system in case the bed of the River Thames was damaged by bomb attack.*

Running late

At every station posters on hoardings cried down 'IS YOUR JOURNEY REALLY NECESSARY', to which most travellers must have answered 'yes', for never were the passenger services so well patronised. People were packed in, completely beyond the capacity of the trains arriving to transport them: soldiers, sailors, airmen, and merchant navy crews, going home on leave or setting off for new postings, workers travelling hundreds of miles to new factories where they had been directed by the Ministry of Labour, normal commuters, and even car-owners forced on to the trains by petrol shortages.

So great was the strain, that trains could not hope to keep to time schedules. More time was added to journeys when threatened air-raids forced trains to pull into stations, for passengers to seek shelter if necessary. On top of this the actual bomb damage which did occur resulted in monumental delays. Commuters travelling into London from the suburbs, could find themselves spending as long in the train as they did at work, whilst cross-country journeys

Above: *Even in the darkest days of war, some people managed to escape from the cities to take a few days holiday, either in the country or by the sea. This traffic added even more pressure to a railway system bursting at the seams. However, people seemed to take the delays with good spirit, as is evidenced in this view outside a refreshment stand at Waterloo on July 31st 1943.*

Right: *Even though delays were inevitable, the railways endeavoured to keep their passengers informed of what was happening. The impersonality of loud-speaker announcements, when services, platform departures and arrival times were continually changing, led to the introduction of information men. The service seemed somehow more personal, more human, as is shown in this view of a London Transport 'Information Man' sparing a few moments for an injured seaman in the bustle at Liverpool Street in November 1940.*

often occupied the best part of 24 hours – with many passengers standing all the way.

Perhaps the worst incident of overcrowding is recorded at Kettering where a woman travelling by train had been taken ill and died; before her body could be removed and the train allowed to progress, 95 people had to be asked by the station-master to get off the train.

Scheduled services were frequently delayed as a priority troop train went through; while in some cases regular passenger trains were simply taken over by the Military Transport Liaison Officers, and the passengers turned out (often at a remote station where only the most basic facilities existed). However, the biggest problem of all was, quite simply

that the stock and locomotives were very often not quite where they should be. This had a multiplying effect; so that even if a service had a clear line to its destination, it could end up being several hours late arriving there, because the train allocated for that journey was still working on another service which had been delayed. When delayed trains finally did arrive, they would often have missed their 'path', and in turn be forced to wait for a clear road. This was overcome wherever possible, with station staff going to extreme lengths to secure an alternative train, even if it was nowhere near adequate for the numbers wishing to travel. In due course, the problem was partially resolved when the Railway Executive introduced a form of coach

pooling which involved almost all of the 46,000 coaches in service.

Above: *If any picture ever told a story, this view at Euston on January 29th 1940 says it all. The atrocious weather of the winter of 1939/40 created numerous problems all over the railway network. A milder spell in mid-January compounded these, when the effects of snow and ice were added to by intense fog which blanketed the whole country. Coupled with the other problems of operating a transport system in wartime, the delays were somewhat inevitable. The chalked slogan on the bottom of the board, reads 'SCOTCH 'UP' TRAINS RUNNING APPROX. 350 MINUTES LATE'.*

Keeping them running

As discussed earlier, the state of Britain's railways in 1938 was one in which the 'Big Four' could take some pride. Their investment programmes in the pre-war years had seen a number of the pre-grouping locomotive classes disappear entirely, with others ready to be phased out. A variety of modernisation programmes in full swing saw new designs in motive power, providing fast streamlined locomotives, workmanlike shunting engines and powerful mixed traffic types. In the early years of the war, the building programme continued with 170 new locomotives entering service in the first six months. Against this 135 were withdrawn, with about 20% of these being scrapped, though in the same six month period 157 locomotives which had been 'in store' or condemned were repaired and returned to work.

Therefore the percentage of new or repaired locomotives was quite high when the number of machines in service peaked at 19,625 in 1942. However the daily toll of high running, limited parts, indifferent coal, and less than desirable maintenance schedules began to take a toll. The loss of skilled workers, replaced by callow apprentices and women, also took its toll until the time they became fully trained. Whilst everyone worked to their maximum, it was not sufficient, and inevitably the machines took the toll. However, a re-build, overhaul, or major service at the works was a luxury denied to many engines. Instead the lot fell on the loco's home shed, where hasty patched jobs were effected in less than ideal surroundings. Foreign engines which failed at a depot were repaired, but generally it was a 'make-do and mend job', barely sufficient to get the locomotive off their hands and back home.

As the war progressed the situation worsened, with depots in the invasion build-up zone (ie mainly the Southern Railway) bearing the brunt of the work. Shed personnel worked hard to turn round failed locomotives, but according to one retired shed superintendent, 'it was always an uphill job, with three locos waiting to take the place of the one you'd repaired'. The volume of work put into maintenance during this period testifies to a superhuman effort, which will never again be repeated on Britain's railways. Hours were extended, with 14 hour days becoming commonplace. For footplate crews this was probably followed by a few snatched hours in distant lodgings if they were lucky. More commonly, a cold empty railway carriage was their lot, unless an accommodating guard would let them rest in front of his stove for an hour or so.

Coupled with this, the vagaries of the British weather had to be contended with, and during the very first winter of the war which turned out to be a major freeze-up, numerous problems were encountered. In the north fog and snow all but brought some routes to a halt, whilst in the south

severe frost resulted in arcing on some of the 3rd-rail electrified systems. Shortages of materials for both running and permanent way departments affected the repairs needed, but always the resources were found just at the last moment. Track was swapped from minor lines and placed on main lines, whilst sleepers from closed lines were cleaned up and re-used in sidings.

Finally, mention should be made of the inter-company transfers which also affected the efficiency of the service. Locomotives were loaned between the companies, with the GWR borrowing large numbers during the early years of the war to replace those 0-6-0s which had been requisitioned by the War Department. To men at sheds in South Wales, Lancashire & Yorkshire Railway or LNWR design tank engines were an unknown quantity and despite very earnest efforts to keep the engines in good order they regularly failed. When it eventually arrived home to its northern shed choice words would be expressed at the abilities of 'foreigners'.

Opposite: *Gresley LNER Class N2 0-6-2T, No 4559, seen shunting in the darkness of a London goods yard in November 1943. Working by the dim light of a shaded lamp, the crews check destination labels, an awkward and difficult task, particularly on rain swept nights.*

Top Left: *As Britain prepared for the invasion of France in 1944, locomotives and crews were worked almost to breaking point. After a few hours respite, the crew of this unidentified LMS Royal Scot 4-6-0 fill tender No 9335 with water at Camden Shed to top up the 4,000 gallons carried by these machines.*

Top Right: *With sunlight filtering through a crack in the shed roof, a re-tubing operation takes place on March 14th 1944, as the build-up to the invasion extends the daily toil.*

Bottom Left: *When this picture of a tired fireman was discovered, there was no information to accompany it . . . but was anything else needed?*

Bottom Right: *When there was no room under cover, engines had to be repaired where they stood as was the case for this fitter and his mate, working on a jammed outside cylinder.*

Women at work

In 1938 around 26,000 women were employed on the railways. Their jobs fell mainly into two categories, clerical and domestic staff: clerks, typists, telephone/telegraph operators, cooks, mess-room attendants, refreshment room staff, carriage cleaners, and crossing keepers. However, by and large it was a male dominated industry, with 650,000 men on the combined payrolls.

At the outbreak of war, it was perhaps understandable that many men wished to enlist in the armed forces. At first only a few were released for war service, including those who were in one of the military reserve forces. A large number of men were in fact reservists for the Royal Engineers, and as soon as they could be released, these railway engineers went overseas to help run Britain's military railway service. Eventually around 103,000 railway employees were released from railway service and went away to war.

To combat the general shortage of manpower, the Ministry of Labour directed women into work on farms, in factories and on the railways. By 1943, the number of women working on the railway peaked at 105,703, with members of the gentler sex being found in almost every avenue of railway service. Now for the first time, a new term 'Railwaywoman' was heard, as women became porters, 'delivery-men', 'signalmen', 'lampmen', station announcers and booking clerks. In addition to these 'light' duties, women were also found at work on much more manual tasks: loading goods trains, oiling and greasing, working on the permanent way staff, driving delivery vans, or at the sheds as loco cleaners and fire-raisers.

On the work-benches, at the sheds and in the railway workshops, they trained to become engineers. Like the men alongside them, they soon learned to undertake skilled work such as core-making, copper-smithing, welding, turning, joinery, and concrete mixing. After a short period of training these 'railwaywomen' were paid the same rate as men doing comparable work. This was largely on the insistence of the rail unions, who fought a lengthy battle for equality in pay. Consequently,

Opposite: *In peacetime, work for Mrs Phelps was found in a mineral water factory, but in September 1942 she was captured on film as an oiler on the Southern Railway; but however did she manage to walk around a railway yard in those shoes?*

Below Top: *The influx of women into the railway service was slow at first, but as more men in 'non-reserved occupations' were called up, they flooded in. The LPTB was amongst the first to retrain women, as in the case of this former Metropolitan Railway employee who is being trained as a booking clerk at Baker Street Station.*

Below Bottom: *Just a few weeks from D-Day, women were much in evidence at London stations helping soldiers to check if their trains were running. Interestingly, this view at Charing Cross shows the work of the official censor, who has removed the badge from the sergeant's sleeve.*

Right: *Training for ticket clerks took just five weeks in the Southern Railway's school, after which girls were sent to a station for two weeks as a 'learner'. After this they were considered qualified, but were doubtlessly watched by the anxious station masters to whom they were assigned.*

these women were well paid by standards of the day. Many were wives of existing railwaymen, or of railwaymen who had enlisted in the armed forces. Additionally many had families, and still had to care for their homes and children after a long day at work. On analysis, it can be safely said that the maintenance of the British railways was in no small part due to the sterling efforts of these women who by the end of the war made up around one sixth of the total employees in the service.

At the end of the war, the majority of women working on the railways left their temporary employment and resumed their peace-time occupations. Some of those who left, later returned and remained at work on the railways for many years, though normally they were engaged only on light duties or clerical grades. A few managed to find permanent work in the industry that had adopted them when the war ended, however by the time of nationalisation in 1948 it was once more a male dominated industry, with women only accounting for about 9.5% of the total workforce.

Opposite Top Left: *Light duties were not the only railway skills learnt by women in the war, as can be seen by this girl working on re-metalling a bearing at Crewe works.*

Opposite Bottom Left: *The Great Central line was built to London in a period of great social change, but the engineers who installed this point rodding would have scarcely believed that its regular maintenance would fall to Mrs Leighton of Nottingham.*

Opposite Right: *By September 1941, over 2,500 women were working in almost every aspect of railway service, just like Catherine Barrat who formerly worked in the Terry's chocolate works at York. Though as her 'temporary' arm band shows, she transferred to driving a LNER delivery van from the local station.*

Right: *It wasn't just working class women who were directed into the railway service, as can be gathered from this picture in London's West End. Fresh from her success as the leading lady in a local theatre, actress Daphne Goodacre pilots her new 'leading man' in her daytime job with the LMS.*

Freight traffic

General freight traffic for both civilian and military needs was regulated by the Ministry of Supply, and managed by Regional Transport Committees. Zoning of supplies, district by district, was introduced, to make each region self-supporting, and therefore partially independent. There was a noted increase in home-produced food encouraged by the 'Dig For Victory' campaign, which saw the establishment of several hundred new regional agricultural schemes. This reduced the number of freight miles considerably, eliminating needless long-distance cross country trips. However, this was balanced out by an increase in freight for home produced items such as sugar beet, tractors, butter and meat, the bulk of which had previously been imported.

Throughout the war years, Britain was heavily dependent on trans-Atlantic convoys to provide it with the necessities of daily life. The stories of the terrible losses suffered by Britain's Merchant Navy have been well documented elsewhere, so it is sufficient to say that they literally kept Britain alive. Once these convoys had arrived at their ports of destination, the job of forwarding the precious cargoes fell on the British railways. The convoy trains were given an immediate priority over most other forms of freight traffic, primarily in order to get the goods away from the dockland areas, which nightly came under heavy aerial attack. Once the goods were loaded onto their respective trains, they were pulled away to 'safe' marshalling points, from where they would be worked onward in the fullness of time.

Another form of freight traffic which developed, emanated from newly built Government factories in rural areas. These factories were the result of a Ministry of Supply policy to build on green-field sites, close to sources

supplying the raw materials used in production. This was a logical move, because often the raw material was heavy whilst the finished product was light. By this strategy, the demand on railway freight movements were reduced by up to 40%, though movements in workers' trains increased by about 26%.

Civilian traffic which had previously been carried by other means, particularly coast-wise shipping, was now forced on to the railways – specifically coal from North-East England which had plied down the east coast to London. By 1943, around 4 million tons of coal were being carried each week, of which about 45% had been moved by coastal shipping in the pre-war years. To handle this traffic, block trains were introduced to run from collieries to distribution centres. Trains were marshalled, with wagons placed in strict order, in an attempt to reduce the amount of marshalling and shunting involved.

Other types of fuel were essential to the national effort, and the country was heavily dependent on imported oil and petroleum products. Long hazardous

Opposite: *Contrasts in mobile freight in Grove Street, Deptford on March 21st 1940. Southern Railway Class E1, No 2215, running bunker first from WD Supply Reserve Depot, passes the Morris Commercial 'Garment Van' which was supplied new to the Co-op Tailoring Factory in Leeds, and is possibly still in their service despite being so far from home. The shaded head lights, and white bands round lamp standards bear mute witness to the black-out regulations.*

Top Right: *Like the Co-op tailoring, firms like Montague Burton were kept busy throughout the war first supplying uniforms, then 'de-mob' suits. Burton's delivery vans, with their Leeds registration plates soon appeared at a number of distribution points based at stations around the country.*

Bottom Right: *The most unusual loads soon began to appear in station yards, replacing the normal peace-time traffic. Heckmondwike Station on the ex-L&YR line from Mirfield to Bradford was used to seeing loads of coal, or woollen cloth in its goods yard, but this view shows the vast amount of barbed wire traffic which was despatched during the war years.*

journeys made by convoys from the middle-east or America saw billions of barrels of oil arriving at ports along the west coast. At an early stage of the war, a number of pipelines were constructed to convey this fuel to distribution centres located well away from the ports. However, despite this, at least 3,000,000 gallons of oil or petrol still had to be moved daily by the railways.

All of these freight movements came at a time when resources were stretched, with the overriding priority being given to military traffic, troop trains etc. Despite these constraints, and a reduction in staff, the railways continued to get the goods through. A major source of traffic in steel making areas were the 'war salvage'

Above: *Prior to 1939, the LNER operated few boat train services, though it would hardly have envisaged that a request for a 'boat train' for the Ministry of Supply would have looked like this load passing through London in August 1942. The location is classified as 'secret' by the official censor, but could it be on the North Woolwich branch?*

Right: *During the London 'blitz' almost 60% of the city's houses were destroyed or badly damaged. In all about 80% required repair at any one time, and to effect these repairs, supplies of raw materials were brought into the city daily. In September 1941, GWR Class 5700 0-6-0PT No 3727 heads for the city passing near Southall carrying timber for the public works departments.*

trains which brought in every conceivable form of scrap iron available – varying from old bedsteads to the railings from civic parks and stately homes.

The necessities of a country at war saw a nation resorting to some very unusual practices, like the burning of peat, use of seaweed in foodstuffs, and the manufacture of 'timber' from pulped paper or sawdust. In the course of these schemes, it fell to the railways to transport these unusual materials to a variety of destinations. One amusing story from this period is that of a non-refrigerated van, which arrived late one Saturday evening in 1943 at a small County Durham station. When opened, it was found to be carrying several boxes of

Above: *To cater for the growing agricultural traffic, new stations, depots and warehouses were opened all over the country, though at Feltwell Fen in East Anglia, a whole new 20 mile stretch of 'light railway' was opened. The 5,000 acre growing area which had defied farmers for years was reclaimed by the Ministry of Agriculture in under a year. The Wissington Light Railway was formally opened by the Minister of Agriculture, Mr Robert Hudson, on July 14th 1941, who is pictured on the footplate of the Manning Wardle 0-6-0T (works No 2006), which bears the headboard 'Bread & Butter Express'.*

Left: *Whether the job was big or small, the railways handled it, as was the case when a complete farm was re-located from the Home Counties to the West Country following the requisition of the farmer's land for an RAF base. Almost the entire siding and platform space was taken up with loaded vans and wagons, when the farm was moved lock, stock and barrel on March 10th 1941.*

ripe bananas, which would have been rotten by the time they were forwarded to the USAF base they were intended for. Consequently, a village which had seen very little foreign fruit since 1939 engaged in an act of community robbery – with a little connived aid from sympathetic LNER employees!

Military freight was the main source of traffic, the complexity of which would fill a book on its own. Basically there were four main peak periods when military freight was at its height: first being the mobilisation of the BEF in 1939, the second being on the evacuation from Dunkirk the following year. In fact the BEF left almost all of its equipment in France, but in the months following Dunkirk all the repatriated units had to be re-equipped with supplies being brought by rail. The next two periods were times when Britain went on the offensive. In 1942 came the despatch of the 1st Army to North Africa, when almost 700 military freights were run in addition to 150,000 wagon loads conveyed on normal freight services. Then came the greatest period of freight working of all,

the prelude to the D-Day landings of June 1944. This time alone saw thousands of extra military freight workings, most of which headed for the military concentration depots which had been created all over the southern counties in the latter part of 1943. Complete goods yards, some capable of holding 2,500 wagons, were constructed on sites where only the barest railway service existed before. From these new yards, vast quantities of stores were eventually shipped out to France: Micheldever depot near Winchester (nicknamed 'Woolworths'), boasted it could supply anything from nuts and bolts to a complete engine for a tank.

Opposite Left: *Dried food became a staple part of the British diet during the war years, with dried milk and powdered egg being the most used. Naturally, it fell to the Railways to move these loads quickly away from their ports of import, but they had to maintain a very strict level of security as there was quite a 'black-market' demand for these goods. On the ration, this dried milk from America and New Zealand sold for around 9d (4p) a can.*

Opposite Right: *With food and consumer goods in such short supply, it seems strange that this load discovered at Euston station in December 1943, went unclaimed. Turkeys, 60 denier stockings and oranges, all worth a king's ransom are being examined by LMS staff, who were probably just part of a small stream of people who would come and stare at these precious items.*

Top Right: *Coal, ever important, was literally Britain's life-blood in the war, and miners were then looked on as heroes. They literally kept the home fires burning, but this unidentified group could still pose for the Camera in January 1943, amidst a crowded yard of coal wagons awaiting despatch.*

Bottom Right: *Imports of oil and petroleum were essential for the vehicles used by both the military and civilians. This precious cargo moved day and night, and even over Christmas 1943 the traffic continued as this view of Cambridge shows: a lengthy train of 'road spirit' tanks passing a local headed by LNER (ex-Great Eastern) F3 2-4-2T No 8075, with a crowded goods yard and shed in the background.*

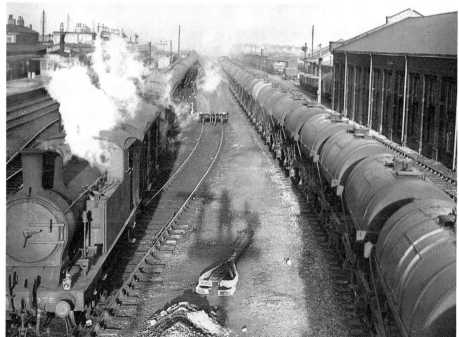

Refreshments

In the pre-war years, rail catering services were at their zenith; trains like the Cornish Riviera Express, Yorkshire Pullman, Coronation Scot, and Golden Arrow represented the last word in passenger luxury. In September 1939, there were almost 900 restaurant cars in regular daily service, with countless station hotels, buffets, dining rooms and the like. However, on the outbreak of war, these services virtually disappeared overnight. The first casualty was the immediate withdrawal of almost all the restaurant cars, whilst at station buffets and hotels, what little food that remained on sale was just the most basic fare.

Within a few months 'Sorry No . . .' notices began to appear. Crockery and cutlery became scarce; in consequence, spoons chained to buffet counters became a common sight. Curious looking sugar was spooned into cracked cups containing a variety of indifferent liquids which respectively passed as tea, coffee, and

Above: *When the Railway executive withdrew buffet and dining cars in September 1939, it also classified stewards who worked in them as available for military service. Consequently, as these services were gradually reintroduced, women had to be employed in their place. In this LNER buffet car, on May 19th 1941, a female 'Steward' draws a drink for servicemen bound for Norwich.*

Right: *To cater for servicemen travelling long-distance, a new form of rail catering was introduced on January 20th 1941. For the first time, travelling canteens were introduced, having been designed to be carried in coach compartments. The meals which cost 10 (old) pence are seen here being officially introduced by Princess Helena Victoria, Colonel Moore-Brabazon (Minister of Transport) and Lord Stamp.*

cocoa. Members of the forces were somewhat better served, usually in special canteens, staffed largely by middle-aged ladies in various uniforms, denoting their membership of the WVS, Red Cross etc.

These canteens were opened whenever a troop train was expected, even in the dead of night, though at some busy stations the canteens were continuously staffed 24 hours a day.

Packed lunch boxes were prepared for both civilian and military passengers, whilst on certain trains restaurant cars were re-introduced from 1940 onwards. Towards the end of the war, a better variety of food was becoming available, and the railway companies made an impressive effort to resume catering standards, despite the rationing of food which still continued. An example of this was the Southern Railway which introduced 12 'Station Maid' tea trolleys. Jointly designed by the Southern and the Empire Tea Bureau, these attractive looking carts plied the platforms of the main Southern stations, taking food to hungry passengers. Even 'cream' cakes, which were now beginning to appear after an absence of six and a half years, reached

the customer in perfect order – each trolley having a specially-sprung covered cake rack!

Above: *When restaurant cars were withdrawn in 1939, packed lunch boxes were supplied to rail travellers. The leisurely personal service in evidence at Euston on September 13th 1939 is in marked contrast with what followed after the 'phoney war' period.*

Left: *The post-war tea trolley appeared on Southern stations early in 1946 and even though heavy rationing was still in force, it provided a standard of luxury unthought of just a few months earlier. Six foot long by three foot six inches wide, it carried four, 3-gallon insulated tea urns, two ice cream cabinets and was electrically driven. Though who can tell if the cream in the cakes is real or artificial?*

Hospital trains

When the Government took control of the railways by The Railway Executive Committee, one of its earliest priorities, was to repeat a course of action it had undertaken successfully during World War I. Then, a number of Ambulance Trains had been ordered for use at home and overseas. Throughout those war years, these trains had ferried their passengers to hospital or repatriation with their families. Several remained in duty until the early 1920s, with the last one being returned to the LMS a few months after the grouping of 1923.

The success of moving injured military personnel by train having thus proved itself, led to the immediate formation of several ambulance trains in 1939. Again they were developed for use either at home or overseas, with formation and numbers of coaches adjusted accordingly. The trains were fully furnished and

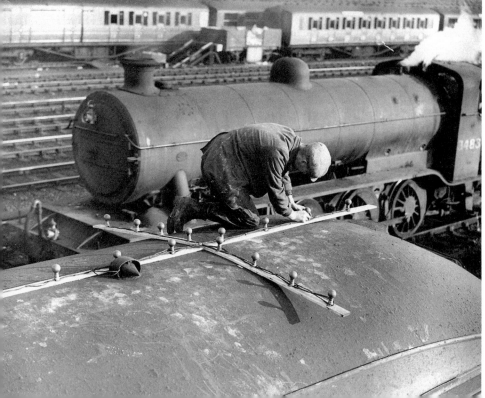

manned by doctors, nurses and ward orderlies. There were wards for both stretcher and sitting cases, with provision to care for mental patients. Kitchens, pharmacies, treatment rooms and even operating theatres were built into the trains. A number of overseas trains were provided with decontamination units, with facilities for disposing of infested clothing, whilst all the trains had the capability to deal with infectious cases. Several vehicles were in fact those constructed for the Great War hospital trains, but the majority were converted coaching stock.

In addition to the ambulance trains, a series of Evacuation Trains were also formed, with 27 having been commissioned by March 1941. These were primarily designed for the evacuation of casualties, carrying them from danger areas to places of safety. They were employed to move hospital patients away from the big cities to cottage hospitals in the countryside, though their conception came from other fears. The threat of gas attacks and mass bombings had convinced the Government that all the major cities in Britain would come under attack, and that the resulting casualty toll would be very high. The primary purpose of the evacuation train was to sit outside the city whilst an attack was in progress, then enter on the 'all clear' to provide an emergency field hospital, which could treat the casualties, and later evacuate them to a place of safety. Fortunately, conditions under which these trains were to be used were not experienced, and because of their value elsewhere a number were made into full ambulance trains or converted for other use.

As with the military freight traffic, use of ambulance and evacuation trains appears to have had specific peaks. These were immediately prior to the evacuation of Dunkirk, following the disastrous raid on Dieppe by Canadian and British Commando forces, after the 'D-Day landings', and in the last months of the war when the final assault was made towards Berlin. In that latter period the trains were not only used to bring home soldiers wounded in the final offensive, but also thousands of emaciated servicemen and civilians who had been liberated from the Nazi concentration camps in Germany, Poland and Austria.

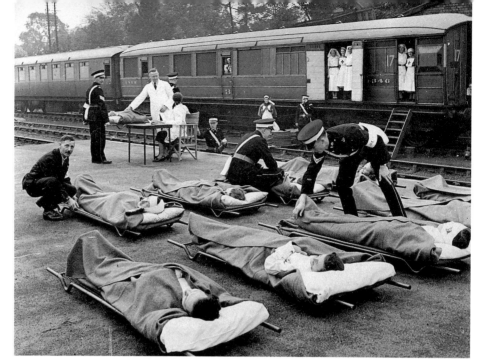

Opposite Top: *The immediate formation of the ambulance trains was handled by the carriage departments of the 'Big Four', with work being carried out as a top priority. Here at Swindon Carriage works, Great Western stock is given the final touches with the painting of 'Geneva' (red) crosses on the roof.*

Opposite Bottom: *By contrast, Ambulance trains supplied by the LNER were furnished with illuminated crosses. This device is being fitted to the roof of an evacuation train on November 24th 1939, as ex-GN Class 02 2-8-0. No 3483 coasts past on an empty van train.*

Top Right: *Two days later the same train officially entered service, and was based on the former GER section. The official commissioning ceremony was accompanied by a demonstration of evacuation techniques using LNER employees as volunteer 'victims'.*

Bottom Right: *One of the 'France' ambulance trains of the British Quartermaster's Unit, at Dover Marine Station on February 7th 1940. The 'Eclipse' sign, complete with cat wearing a bowler hat, boots and spats, originated from the words of a famous army song.*

Luggage

With the tremendous movement of military and civilian personnel during the period 1939-45, another strain was put on the railway networks. Strangely, it is the side of railway operations that is rarely discussed, but one which no railway system would ever operate without – passengers' luggage. Almost every station in the land had facilities for handling luggage, varying from small cupboards at tiny country stations to vast basement rooms extending beneath the main-line termini.

Luggage was basically in two types: personal items carried on the train journey with the passenger, or luggage sent in advance at a much reduced rate. At the outbreak of war Britain's railways were handling around 50 million pieces of

Top: *'Find the porter': King's Cross September 14th 1944, with the left luggage room brimming with a huge collection of prams and bicycles. This huge collection was the result of an unauthorised and large scale return of evacuees, despite the Government's empassioned 'Stay away for the present' warnings.*

Left: *Manchester Central Station on June 23rd 1940, with a Post Office official helping sort a mountain of parcels. Almost the entire mountain is comprised of packages of civilian clothing being returned home by men who have 'joined up' in the armed forces.*

Opposite: *The temporary left luggage cloakroom, established at Fenchurch Street Station, was typical of hundreds of others at stations up and down the country. These depositories differed from normal luggage offices in that they were intended just for members of HM Forces. Here they could leave almost any item of kit, except great coats, for 24 hours free of charge. Weapons could also be checked in, as is exampled by this fresh faced soldier handing over his rifle, without anyone giving it a second glance. The age of the soldiers in the foreground illustrates the age at which young men were expected to fight and even lay down their lives for King and Country: October 22nd 1942.*

advance luggage a year, with an additional 75 million pieces being stored in left luggage offices for periods over 12 hours. At the outbreak of war the 'luggage in advance' service was withdrawn, though passengers could still send on trunks, suitcases etc by the standard luggage service. Unfortunately no statistics appear to have been kept for the period of the war years, but it is conceivable that even with the restrictions the figures shown above would have doubled or even trebled.

One form of luggage which became a common site at the stations during the early months of the war, were the 'civvies': clothes and personal effects which were being sent home by men enlisting in the forces. Inside a few months the standard issue, navy, and air-force blue kit bags began to appear in their stead, as servicemen moved around the country carrying their essential belongings with them.

In fact the kit bag became synonymous with railway travel; for it also doubled as something to sit on in coaches where all the seats were taken, or on crowded platforms where men had to wait for trains which could be running up to several hours late. To avoid congestion on passenger trains, certain restrictions were imposed to regulate the amount of luggage which could be carried by each person. Inevitably these rules failed, because guards turned a 'blind eye', or because people were unwilling to send luggage ahead unaccompanied (when it might easily be lost for days on end). Eventually the problem was in part resolved by the coupling of a passenger-rated goods van to many passenger trains.

Armament traffic

The movement of military traffic during the war years was both intensive, and of course highly classified. Even with the freedom of information now afforded fifty years on, full details are difficult to find. Therefore only a generalisation can be made concerning this traffic, whose full details if available would probably fill an entire book. The size, scope and variety of military traffic during the war years can only be hinted at though the accompanying selection of photographs which only show part of the diversity of military loads carried on Britain's railways. The vast majority of loads went 'under wraps', and in many instances with even the locomotive crews not knowing what they were carrying.

Some consignments were impossible to conceal inside goods vans or under wagon sheets, so larger items were often crated or loaded in packing cases. Where this was not possible, the loads would often be disguised, or their appearance altered in some respects in order to confuse any information which might be gained by the enemy, either through aerial reconnaissance or from their agents in Britain.

Above: *Twelve inch naval guns, bound for shipyards on the Clyde, are seen leaving for the north on specially designed LNER wagons on May 10th 1944, as Britain prepares to open 'the second front'.*

Below: *A number of freight-concentration depots were opened at strategic locations in the south of England. When the Allies were ready to invade France, it would* need its own railway system, and this picture taken on February 23rd 1944, shows one of the biggest 'train sets' of all time. Everything that would be needed for operating a railway in France, locomotives, coaches, weapons, hospital trains, and even refrigerated food vans, were assembled for shipping in pre-fabricated kit form.

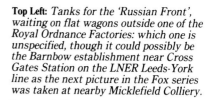

Top Left: *Tanks for the 'Russian Front', waiting on flat wagons outside one of the Royal Ordnance Factories: which one is unspecified, though it could possibly be the Barnbow establishment near Cross Gates Station on the LNER Leeds-York line as the next picture in the Fox series was taken at nearby Micklefield Colliery.*

Bottom Left: *Instantly recognisable, the LMS carriage and wagon works, Derby, with one of the biggest orders ever out-shopped. This train of eight, 12-inch rail mounted howitzers was just one of the 'secret' orders produced by the 44,000 employees in LMS workshops around the country. December 12th 1944.*

Bottom Right: *Cleckheaton Junction, at Mirfield on the ex-LYR 'Spen Valley' line, with the main trans-Pennine line to Leeds in the background. A secret load of crated supplies for Russia on March 3rd 1942, is held whilst yard-men check wagon ropes. From the stencilled identification numbers on each packing case, the crates would seem to be holding 'Bren Gun Carriers' and would probably have originated from either Huddersfield, Sheffield or Penistone.*

Accidents

Despite the intensity of traffic movements, the war years were relatively accident free. Several incidents occurred as a result of bomb damage to tracks and stations, but these are not officially recorded as accidents. Of those true railway accidents which did occur, the following were among the most serious. Shortly after the outbreak of war, a rear-end collision occurred near Bletchley on October 13th 1939 when the 7.50 Euston to Stranraer ran into the back of the 7.37 Euston to Inverness. The following March a more traditional type of accident happened between Aviemore and Carr Bridge, when the failure of a drawbar resulted in 21 wagons and brake-van running away backwards and colliding with a Perth-Inverness freight killing the driver and fireman.

An unusual event took place at Wembley Central in October 1940, when a station barrow being taken down a ramp ran away and became wedged on the running line. It was struck by the 11.50am Liverpool-Euston express, which was de-railed with a number of passengers killed and about 50 injured. A few weeks later, on November 4th 1940, one of the most serious rail accidents of the war occurred at Norton Fitzwarren on the GWR. A driver on a Paddington-Penzance train misread the signals and ran into trap points, leaving 26 dead and 56 injured.

At Harold Wood on February 10th 1941, the driver of a Liverpool Street-Southend passenger train ran into the rear of the preceding express to Norwich. Four months later a head on collision resulted when a Plymouth-Paddington express met a west-bound freight on the same section of track near Slough on July 2nd. This was followed by a side to side collision at Eccles on December 8th, when the Rochdale-Pennington local service over-ran signals after the premature suspension of 'fog working', and collided with another local passenger train from Kenyon to Manchester.

In 1942 two major accidents occurred, the first being at Beighton on the former Great Central line, when a troop train struck a misplaced load on a freight train.

A load of steel sheet had slipped so badly that it was out of gauge, and fouling the opposite running line, the resulting collision claimed the lives of 16 servicemen. On November 13th at Appleford, near Didcot on the GWR, the midnight Paddington to Birkenhead ran into several derailed wagons from a goods train, claiming the lives of four people aboard the express. The following year seems remarkably accident free, with the only major accident reported, caused by the collapse of a locomotive firebox at Honeybourne near Worcester. It involved a USA 2-8-0, allocated to the GWR:

The final year of the war, when traffic was at its height, was relatively free from major accidents; though one occurred at Esher on January 28th 1945, when an electric train from Waterloo to Portsmouth collided with a steam hauled train to Bournemouth due to a signalman's error.

Though not a frequent occurrence, it was quite common for sparks from locomotive chimneys to set fire to combustible material in open wagons they were hauling. When these wagons contained explosives the situation was critical, though despite the amount of military traffic carried between 1939 and 1945, only three accidents stand out in their severity when the trains involved literally blew themselves up. The first happened on June 2nd 1944 when a wagon behind a WD 2-8-0 No 7337 carrying bombs for the USAF caught fire at Soham, Cambridgeshire. The crew did all they could to avert the destruction of the town though the fireman, and the local signalman were both killed and the station raised to the ground. A similar incident occurred nine months later, when a LMS 0-6-0 4F carrying a load of sea mines to Carnforth caught fire at Bootle in Cumbria, the resulting explosion killed the driver and injured the fireman and the guard. The third accident occurred just three weeks later near Selby in Yorkshire when a number of 500lb bombs exploded, though this time it was the driver of a passing train who was killed. In each of these instances, when the crews discovered the fire, they made courageous efforts to uncouple the blazing wagon from the rest of the train, thus reducing the danger of the whole train exploding.

Opposite Top: *Five people, including three sailors going home on leave from the naval base at Plymouth, were killed when the 6.20pm express to Paddington crashed near Slough. Unfortunately, the express' progress was impeded when it collided head on with a goods train on the same section of track. Of particular interest is the Military Liaison Officer standing in the foreground surveying the urgent work of clearing the main line.*

Opposite Bottom: *Almost total devastation, caused not by a bomb or the result of enemy action, but by the simple, though tragic, case of a station barrow running away and fouling the running line: the aftermath is seen at Wembley Central on October 13th 1940, with LMS Patriot Class 5XP 4-6-0 No 5529, completely over on one side, with its 3,500 gall Fowler tender No 4495, at right angles to the cab. In the background, the shattered remains of a parachute water tank which once stood at the end of the platform are seen in front of a 'pooled' wagon which had formerly belonged to Dundee Corporation.*

Below: *In complete contrast to the cover picture, LNER Class B12 4-6-0 No 8556 lays in a sorry dejected state after being involved in a collision near Brentwood. The accident occurred in February 1941, when a Liverpool Street-Southend train crashed into the back of a stationary Liverpool Street-Norwich express.*

Locos for abroad

Initially the immediate needs of the WD were met by commandeering locomotives from the 'Big Four', with 0-6-0 types being particularly popular. However, many of the 2-8-0 ex-ROD locomotives (to a former Great Central Railway design) from the First World War, which were still giving sterling service on some main line railways were initially refused by the Ministry when offered to them, though a few later saw service in the middle-East. Instead the WD resorted to ordering new machines for service in France. In the following months, the Ministry of Supply placed orders for 240, 2-8-0s to the Stanier 8F design modified with air brake equipment for overseas use. Two orders for 100 locomotives were placed respectively with Beyer Peacock, and the North British Loco Co, whilst the remaining 40 were ordered from the Vulcan Foundry.

Meanwhile the requisitioned locos were shipped out to the continent through Harwich, Hull and Felixstowe. Several of the ex-GWR Dean Goods 0-6-0s passed through Ipswich in November 1939, painted in a dull-black livery with pale yellow 'WD' lettering. Unfortunately, the BEF was forced to retreat from France before most of the new locos could be

delivered, these were then re-assigned for use in other theatres of war.

Further batches of the Stanier design were ordered throughout the war for use in Britain, with members of the class being built by all four British companies. Most were given the LMS markings of their designing company, but some were regarded as LNER stock and marked accordingly.

The supply of standard British designs to countries as diverse as Turkey and Egypt may seem strange, when compared with what was happening elsewhere on Britain's railways. On the Great Western, shortages of motive power were creating considerable problems, and in turn Britain had to seek overseas aid in order to keep its railways running. So on December 11th 1942, the whistle of an American locomotive was heard when the first main line steam engine was handed over at Paddington Station. Though these engines were actually intended for use overseas, a number of them began handling traffic which had previously been in the charge of British locos now working abroad. After the war a number of American 0-6-0Ts were taken in to British stock, and many remained in service almost to the end of steam on the Southern Region.

In 1943, the Ministry of Supply's own machines ('utility' engines built to a design by R A Riddles) began to appear.

There were two major types: a 2-8-0 with 4ft 8in driving wheels, and a tractive effort of 34,215lbs; and a somewhat similar but less numerous 2-10-0 type of almost identical power but which, at 78 tons 6cwt, weighed 8 tons 1cwt more than the 2-8-0s. Additionally a powerful 0-6-0ST was designed, primarily for work as a shunting engine. These locomotives

were also sent to a variety of countries overseas, as well as being put into service in Britain. After the war large numbers were shipped back to Britain, and put into store before eventually being taken over by the newly nationalised British Railways in 1948, with 733 2-8-0 and 25 2-10-0s entering service to replace many of the prematurely worn-out members of the British fleet.

Opposite Top: *In addition to the engines ordered by the Ministry of Supply to the Stanier 8F design, a number of LMS machines were requisitioned for service in Persia for the supply route to Russia. On November 13th 1941, No 8031 is seen at Crewe whilst being modified for overseas service. The buffer beam is being altered, but the largest modification of all is the conversion to oil burning.*

Opposite Below: *Having been modified the engines stand in ex-works condition awaiting trans-shipment by hazardous convoy routes to their destination. This would see a number of the class being lost below the sea, including four which were aboard the SS Pentridge Hall sunk in June 1942. These powerful locos weighed in at 72 tons 5cwt when introduced by Stanier in 1935, however these machines had increased in weight by 4½ tons by their conversion. However, at the same time the tractive effort was reduced from 32,440lb to 31,955lbs.*

Top Right: *WD locomotives to the design by R A Riddles wait to be shipped to the continent on March 13th 1945; the majority appear to be 2-8-0 machines. Alongside stand a number of 55 ton 10cwt tenders, already loaded with coal. Also in the same shipment, but not in this view were a number of Ministry of Supply 0-6-0STs which were also constructed to Riddles' design.*

Bottom Right: *Whilst British workshops were turning out machines for use overseas, Britain was importing locomotives from America. As part of a publicity exercise the first of these 'freight' engines was handed over in an official ceremony at Paddington on December 11th 1942. Colonel Ryan, Chief of Transportation for the American Army, is seen here pointing out some of the unusual features to Lord Leathers and Major General J C H Lee.*

The railway works

In the preceding chapters, mention has been made about locomotive sheds being forced to carry out repairs and overhauls that would by rights have been carried out at the works. The reason for this was two-fold: firstly the necessity to keep engines in service at their home sheds, but mainly due to the reduced capacity of the works themselves.

This reduction in capacity was again brought about for two reasons: one that the works were busy constructing WD locomotives for use overseas, the other that the works were being directed to construct other items for the war effort. This situation applied equally at the private railway contractors, as it did in the workshops of the 'Big Four' companies. Firms like the North British found themselves manufacturing bomb casings, whilst another was ordered to construct naval life-boats.

One reason for the direction of capacity at the workshops was a result of their technical excellence. The works were amongst the finest heavy engineering shops in the country, and in terms of quality and skill they were unrivalled, facets which were vital for a nation struggling to maintain its independence.

The work directed to railway workshops was of the widest variety, as is testified by the entry from the order book of Cowans Sheldon in June 1940. Machine six rafts (Admiralty); Machine four screws; Construct two O/head Cranes

Above: *One of the light armoured personnel carriers manufactured at four railway workshops in Britain: two in Scotland and two in England. Based on a Canadian Army design, these fast moving, semi-amphibious machines were maufactured in large numbers during 1941-2, and were used in both Europe and North Africa.*

Below: *Britain's railway workshops turned out some amazing pieces of engineering during the war years, but none would have been as strange as this walking bridge. These 'unit construction bridges' were supplied to the Royal Engineers who used them to replace conventional bridges destroyed by the retreating enemy. One feature of this December 1944 view is the barrage balloon in the distant sky.*

(Admiralty – Singapore); Construct four, 1 Ton Capstans (Air Ministry); 400 Cupola Covers to be machined (Vauxhall Motors); Machine sample buffer cylinder (Ministry of Supply); machine 4,000 Screwed Bases (David Brown & Sons); Repair two coal hoists (LNER); construct 25ton floating crane (Admiralty, Newcastle); Press and assemble 250 Mortar containers (Ministry of War, India Office).

The above is just a random sample of one week at just one works, but the same story must have been repeated all around the country, with the work-load being spread to as many different centres as possible. In adopting this technique, the Ministries of War and Supply avoided 'putting all their eggs in one basket', and production was kept up, even if one factory was put out of action by a bomb attack. So throughout the war years, railway workshops were kept busy constructing bailey bridges, floating docks, tanks, munitions, aircraft, naval vessels, and a whole host of other machined components. However, locomotive building was not overlooked, and throughout the war, engines for use at home and overseas were turned out in their hundreds.

Above: *Despite the diversity of work being undertaken in the railway workshops, it was still 'business as usual' as new machines were outshopped. A feature of the war years was the continuing appearance of members of the LMS 'Coronation' Class. June 27th 1940,* King George VI *receives finishing touches before the naming ceremony.*

Left: *Not only were young boys and women employed in the railway workshops, but skilled engineers past the age of retirement went back to work – some as old as 80. Mr Sylth, seen at work on bomb casings in a north London railway works, had previously applied his engineering skills as a jeweller and watchmaker.*

Right: *The training of some women as engineers was easier than others, those who had formerly worked as dress-makers and machinists seemed to adapt quicker than those who had worked in other professions. On June 15th 1940, a woman pupil receives instruction before going on to work at a north London loco depot.*

With the outbreak of war, the Railway Executive had taken control of the various railway workshops around the country as they had done in World War I. Obviously it is difficult to give even a brief account of all the output in the period 1939-45, but it is worthwhile recording a few features. One immediate effect of Government control was the institution of a ban on the construction of express locomotives, limiting the companies to the manufacture of mixed traffic or freight types. The need for this was clearly seen on the LNER, who found themselves in immediate difficulties over their motive power position at the outbreak of war. Though they had an abundance of express and local types, there was a great absence of mixed traffic locomotives. Fortunately, the Gresley Class V2 2-6-2s were to prove to be tremendous maids of all work, but the building programme allowed for a much needed supplement with Thompson's class B1 4-6-0 of which over 200 were produced between 1942 and 1946. These mixed traffic engines were well appreciated on the former Great Eastern section and saw extensive service on military trains throughout the area, however due to their wide route availability they roamed far and wide.

To meet the need for all forms of motive power, the LMS immediately ceased its scrap and build programme, and began repairing aged locomotives such as the superheated 0-8-0 G1s. Refurbishment of a variety of older classes was achieved simultaneously to the production of the new Stanier types such as the 5MT and 8F. The Southern, like the LNER, were also in need of modern mixed traffic locomotives. This was resolved with the production of two strikingly different locomotive classes, the handsome Merchant Navy 4-6-2 Pacifics and the ungainly Class Q1 0-6-0 tender engines. The latter being a product of the necessity for an engine with a powerful tractive effort coupled to a maximum weight restriction of 54 tons. On the GWR the production of the successful Halls was continued, but with Collett's retirement in 1941 a number of significant changes were made to the class by Hawksworth. Production

of the Class 2251 0-6-0 tender engines continued, but 0-6-0PTs were far more numerous, with over 135 being built between 1940 and 1944. In addition to conventional locomotives, the GWR resumed the production of its diesel railcars planned before the war - two of which were loaned to the LNER for use around Newcastle.

The military need was for heavy freight locomotives, of which the 2-8-0 type had proved itself to be of excellent ability during the 1914-18 conflict. Of these the most significant was Robinson's ROD 2-8-0 (see page 41). The majority of those that were returned were sold to the LNER, with a smaller number going to the GWR. But, with the outbreak of hostilities it was expected that the 300 engines still in service would, once again, be requisitioned by the War Department as a stop gap measure - as it was, the immediate need did not arise during the 'phoney war' period. Meanwhile work had been commenced on an order for modern WD 2-8-0s to the LMS Class 8F designed by William

Stanier in 1935. The engines ordered for the WD benefited from a number of improvements to assist war service, including thicker frames, though production was not solely confined to the LMS workshops. The first examples were ready by 1940, but with the fall of France most were given LMS running numbers and put to work on British railways. Ninety were ordered from Swindon Works, but the last batch of 10 was cancelled. Having built the 80 engines, the GWR made good use of them until it began receiving supplies of the American S160s. The Southern works at Ashford, Brighton and Eastleigh turned out in excess of 150 WD 8Fs, whilst over 100 were built at Doncaster and Darlington before the railways began concentrating on the production of the Austerity 2-8-0s.

Rolling stock manufacture was quite limited, with an embargo being placed on coaching stock production. Early in the war the railway workshops of Britain converted a large quantity of coaching stock in order to form 25 hospital trains, of which twelve were designated for use in Britain. However, on the fall of Europe nine of the overseas trains were lost, which necessitated the construction of a further 33 14-coach ambulance trains for use in Europe after the opening of the second front. This number included conversion of some of the evacuation trains discussed earlier. The first of the new overseas ambulance trains was handed over by the GWR at a special ceremony in March 1943. More special coaching stock work included the provision of special trains for VIPs. For example a train was converted for Winston Churchill's mobile HQ., which was named *Cutlass* (later changed to *Rugged*). General Dweight D. Eisenhower, Supreme Commander of the allied forces had a Swindon-built train with the code name *Alive,* whilst that built at Doncaster for General Montgomery, Commander-in-Chief Home Forces, was designated *Rapier.* In the latter stages of the war a new train, known as *Bayonet* was constructed by the LNER for use by other VIPs, many of whom tended to be American Generals that were stationed in Britain.

As is mentioned elsewhere in this book, wartime maintenance of locomotives and rolling stock was at an all time low, so routine jobs such as carriage refurbishment and painting obviously took a very low priority. On the GWR only the King and Castle classes retained their green livery, whilst only that stock in regular use on the Cornish Riviera or Torbay expresses had repaints in the normal chocolate and cream livery. Elsewhere the coaches were painted a dark brick red colour based on a bauxite resin, whilst locomotives received an unlined black. On the LNER the incoming Edward Thompson who succeeded Gresley in 1941 introduced a form of austere lettering on the side of his locomotives, with the abbreviated N E being displayed instead of the full title - some commentators at the time viewed this as being a symbolism of Thompson's pre-Grouping allegiances, to the North Eastern Railway.

It is also worth recording that, as in World War I, the railway workshops did a great deal of essential war work which was not in anyway connected with their normal activities. Swindon, for example built barrage balloon equipment, 2,000lb and 4,000lb bomb cases and miniature submarines. On the LMS, Covenanter tanks were designed and built at Crewe, Wolverton Carriage Works and Derby produced wings for Lancaster bombers and other aircraft sections, whilst the ex-L&YR shops at Horwich were churning out large

An internal view in 1940 at the Cowans, Sheldon factory at Carlisle which is mentioned in the text. A variety of components are seen inside the St. Nicholas Works, with parts for a 3-ton crane (Admiralty, Gosport), 10-ton Capstans (Admiralty, Sheerness) and a 60ft. turntable for the LMS at Colne being amongst the items which are readily identifiable
NEI COWANS - BOYD PLC.

During the war years the private railway workshops were inordinately busy, with huge order books and an ever-increasing demand. This resulted in a big speed-up of locomotive production, for use both at home and overseas. In what is believed to be the Vulcan works, a locomotive bound for the Indian sub-continent is pictured on final test. The date is March 6th 1940
ATLANTIC COLLECTION

quantities of war items including Matilda tanks. The Barassie Works in Scotland was used to repair Spitfires and an airstrip was created on the neighbouring golf course in order to allow the repaired planes to be flown off direct to their commissioning aerodromes. The LNER also made aeroplane parts at Gorton and Cowlairs whilst Doncaster and York made gliders; Shildon produced ball bearings and gun mountings, whilst manufacturing capacity was well used for the war effort at the other shops. The Southern's works did a lot of vital work for the Royal Nay, in particular Eastleigh and Ashford, whilst their facilities on the Isle of Wight were used to repair naval launches and air sea rescue craft. The Southern also did some invaluable work for Trinity House who were charged with providing extra bouyage to mark wrecks and protect dangerous coastlines after lighthouses were prohibited from fulling their principal function.

Left: *As discussed in the text, the railway companies produced a number of special trains for VIPs such as Churchill, Eisenhower and so on. All were well-appointed and not dissimilar to the Royal Train in many ways. This official Doncaster works view reveals the interior of General Eisenhower's train with all its sumptuous fittings.*
NATIONAL RAILWAY MUSEUM

Right: *Bearing in mind that during war time conditions many long held conventions were thrown to the wind, the development of Bullied's Class Q1 0-6-0 was not such a strange position to take. True, the look of the locomotive may not have been aesthetically pleasing, but it did follow a logical design approach and certainly met the requirements of the Southern during the war. The design, whilst omitting such things as running plates splashers and heavy boiler casing, did utilise many standard parts, patterns and forgings. Bulleid discarded everything which was not essential and ended up with an engine which, whilst looking half finished, was dependable in service and well liked by its crews.*
NATIONAL RAILWAY MUSEUM

Dunkirk

The capitulation of the Belgian army in the north and the sudden thrust of the German armoured divisions to the south unexpectedly cut off the BEF and their French allies, to the extent that retreat back across the channel from Dunkirk was the only available option. Mention of this incident, code named Operation Dynamo, automatically brings to mind the heroic actions of the flotilla of 850 vessels which crossed the Channel to help repatriate the stranded forces between May 27th and June 4th 1940. In the armada of ships which took the troops off the beaches, there was an appreciable contingent from the railway-owned shipping fleets. The GWR's *St. Helier* made no less than seven trips to Dunkirk, bringing back nearly 12,000 people and shooting down one enemy plane in the process - even the tiny little *Mew* which usually plied between Dartmouth and Kingswear set off to take part and proceeded to Dover at a speed of no less than 10 knots.

Because Dunkirk was such a major incident it often overshadows other contemporary events of this era. For example, little mention is made of the evacuation from St. Valery-en-Caux in Brittany shortly afterwards; yet in this evacuation, the ships of the Southern Railway and the GWR also took a significant and heroic part. Similarly, mention should be made of the work of the LNER steamers which played a substantial role in the evacuation of Rotterdam. Of these the *St. Dennis* was trapped in the

Most of the repatriated troops were exhausted, dirty and completely without kit, many were covered in salt rime, having been forced to stand in long queues off the Dunkirk beaches whilst awaiting transport. Obviously, food clothing, and a good clean up were in order for the 200,000 British soldiers and about 120,000 French combatants. To facilitate this small supplies of food were handed out before the troops embarked onto their trains as pictured here at Dover Marine Station on June 4th. However, aid which could be provided at the channel ports was limited so a number of stations on the LMS and GWR systems were designated receiving stations, places like Leicester even had ablution blocks set up on the station platforms to cater for the 242 troop trains which passed through the city that June. NATIONAL RAILWAY MUSEUM

harbour and had to be scuttled by her crew who only just managed to get away on the last British destroyer to leave Holland.

However, even less importance is attached to what happened to the troops and civilians who were dumped on the quaysides or beaches of England once they had been brought safely back. Yet, in view of the fact that invasion might quickly follow this retreat, it was left to the Railway Executive to clear the coastal areas as quickly as possible. Planning for the possible withdrawal of repatriated personnel had begun as early as 1938, but it was not realised until the fall of Norway how serious the situation would be if the Germans overran France so quickly. Accordingly, a pool of 186 trains was designated for the evacuation. Naturally, most of the work devolved upon the Southern Railway, but they had to quickly disperse these trains outside their territory. The emergency evacuation trains discussed earlier were immediately pressed into service, with all 34 sets being used in some way following the evacuation from Dunkirk. Twenty of these trains had been stabled for the evacuation of London, so these were readily at hand, but others had been sent to provincial cities and took a little longer in getting to the

During the week and a half that followed Dunkirk the Executive ran no less than 565 military specials 'and handled around 330,000 people.

Associating the evacuation from France with the exhausted and demoralised military forces alone (as shown in the left picture) would be quite wrong, as there was a considerable number of civilians who were carried across the channel in the spring of 1940. Quite incredible to report, as late as April, the British Government were stating that reciprocal travel between England and France should not be discouraged. Accordingly, it is not surprising to find firms like Thomas Cook were advertising inclusive holidays to Paris, Cannes and the Jura. However, by Whitsuntide all such travel was summarily cancelled and people abroad were urged to return home as soon as possible. In addition to British nationals, hundreds of refugees came over the channel, many of whom had never been much further than a few miles from their homes. Despite the language barrier, the bottom picture shows how officials of the Southern Railway endeavour to assist this French civilian at Margate.
BOTH NATIONAL RAILWAY MUSEUM

channel ports which were receiving the repatriated BEF.

Noted railway historian O.S. Nock commented; 'There was frequently no clear idea of where the trains would be eventually routed.' It is certainly true that there were no written working notices, and destinations were organised entirely by telephone. Many went to camps on the GWR system, such as those set up round Oxford, whilst the LMS saw large scale movements into the West Midlands, the North West and into Scotland, by contrast the LNER had fewer trains because the potential for invasion was greater on the eastern side. However at least two were run all the way up the ECML to Aberdeen, whilst considerable use was made of the old Great Central line to take the evacuees up into the East Midlands and beyond.

The trains were made up of ten coaches, because whatever motive power was available such trains would be within its capability. This of course was an important consideration, when one recalls that the GWR loading gauge was too generous to allow the majority of their engines on to the Southern beyond Redhill, Accordingly places like Basingstoke, Reading and Winchester Junction were common exchange points. Meanwhile, during the nine days an increasing number of GWR moguls and Manors were seen on Southern metals.

Receiving the evacuees

The Munich crisis in September 1938 had prompted a fear that Germany might actually start a bombing campaign on Britain without declaring war. As London was assumed to be the primary target, it was decided that the evacuation of the city should not be commenced from the main termini, as these could easily become primary targets for the enemy. Accordingly it was decided that children would be moved by bus or tube, in school groups, to stations on the outskirts such as Ealing Broadway on the GWR and New Barnett on the LNER. With the evacuation of children·being an immediate priority of the Railway Executive once war was declared, the movement of children from the cities to safer country areas had begun on September 1st and continued until around the 25th of that month. The haste in which children were evacuated was commented upon in the first volume of Britain's Railways At War, and a number of readers took me to task on saying that the operation was not well organised. They further pointed out that the railways'

organisation was superb. With trains being loaded and despatched on average every nine minutes from some stations (for example, the GWR handled 58 trains on the first day alone), one has to agree. However, the point still stands that there was massive chaos at the receiving end, where harassed railway officials, billeting officers, school teachers and other voluntary groups like Red Cross and the Women's Voluntary Service were left to pick up the pieces. In response to that first book, well over 100 people wrote to me care of the publishers telling of their difficult and often harrowing experiences:- some of these now follow.

Some of the evacuees who had been moved to the country were able to take advantage of the extreme cold spell which affected the country. One teacher who had taken school children from the Lewisham area to Barnstaple wrote to me of her experiences in taking children such a long way, reporting that 'the melancholy remained amongst the little ones no matter what the teachers and their adoptive parents tried to do. Christmas was a particularly bad time, though some of the better off parents managed to afford the visitors tickets (on

special excursion trains laid on by the Government) and come down to join their children for the holidays. After they had gone things went from bad to worse, until one day we found that the River Taw had been frozen over completely, within a few days the children were able to join locals and go out skating on the ice. School was closed because of the weather, so I organised I a ramble over the river, and we returned back to Barnstaple on the train from Wrafton. After that children learned that life by the seaside could be great fun, and things never seemed quite as black again.'

As an immediate consequence of the defeat of the BEF and the subsequent fall of France, there was again a major displacement of people which the Railway Executive had to organise transport for. The previous section has detailed how the troops were handled after the fall of France, but this necessitated yet another move for the young evacuees who had been moved out of London and other major cities and located in East Anglia, Kent and along the southern coast. As these were now considered the principle invasion areas (as demonstrated in railway terms by the allocation of armoured trains to these areas), it was obviously unwise to leave the young evacuees in areas which might very shortly become militarised zones. One of the expectant mothers who had been evacuated, former GWR rating clerk Rosie Summers, states 'even the second evacuation was attended by problems, as once again it seems that government planning and railway scheduling did not work hand in hand.'

A former head teacher of Thomas Hardy School wrote to me recounting, 'When we left Ipswich the whole school, about 320 in total, was accommodated in just the one train. However,

The dread of aerial attacks on our major towns and cities had prompted the evacuation of 1939, when plans were made to take vulnerable people out of the industrial heartlands of Britain. Many of the movements from the towns and cities were accomplished by busing children to out-laying or suburban stations, in case those in the city centres were bombed. This was a sensible precaution, because as seen on pages 84-5, we have already gained an impression of what could happen to stations which received a direct hit, but such dangers were not solely confined to the capital. For example, a raid on Wearside caused considerable dislocation to railway services on September 6th 1940, when the LNER station at Sunderland received a direct hit.
LNER Official Photograph, courtesy David
JENKINSON COLLECTION.

when we got back to the outskirts of London the children were appalled at the bomb damage they saw and we had a most arduous task consoling them. We were then taken by bus to Willesden and hastily hurried into a line of about 28 carriages standing at the platform, half of which were already full. Some of the older pupils and one junior master were sent down to the front of the train whilst the rest of us settled into the back. What we did not know was that the train was in two halves, and the boys up front were taken off north towards Shrewsbury and we were not even aware of this until we arrived in Northampton. We were never re-united with those children until March 1945 when the school was brought back together again.' A lady from Glasgow recalls a similar incident with her school, when they were split up with her and ten other children arriving at Inverness, whilst her younger sister went to Fort William. Tommy Jays from East Ham was one of the boys sent from Felixstowe to Ystalyfera in South Wales. His journey took two days, necessitating an overnight stay in the station waiting room at Monmouth whilst the girls were taken to sleep in a Boy Scout hut nearby.

Mrs. Annabel James related her infant class was moved no less than three times, first to

Television presenter, Michael Aspel recalls his evacuation from London, that 'it was as if the Pied Piper had come back. The scene had changed from Hamelin to South London, and the River Weser, deep and wide, was now the Wandle, which was narrow and smelled.' With their clothes in battered suitcases or wrapped in stiff brown paper tied up with string, gas mask in cardboard boxes around their necks, the children trooped to stations all around London, such as these pictured here at Surbiton.
NATIONAL RAILWAY MUSEUM

The LMS share in the evacuation of children was extensive, during the first four days of September 1939, they moved $\frac{1}{3}$ million people in 1,450 special trains. From London they ran 160 trains, with 115 from cities in the western division and 45 trains originating from the Midland division. Bradford, Leeds, Manchester, Liverpool, Sheffield, Glasgow and Edinburgh all witnessing extensive movements. This view showing children being evacuated from Liverpool after the blitz there in 1940 is typical of what went on around the country in those days. So poor were many of the children evacuated from this city, that they became nicknamed 'The Kids From Plimsoll City', because their footwear was so woefully inadequate for winter life in rural areas to which they were sent.
LIVERPOOL CITY ENGINEER'S DEPARTMENT

Above: *From all over the seaside districts on the south and east coast another mass evacuation began in the early summer of 1940. On the Great Eastern section of the LNER, trains were on the move, travelling from places like Clacton, Felixstowe and Lowestoft whilst the Southern handled large numbers of trains from seaside towns like Brighton, Deal, Eastbourne, Hastings and Worthing. The distances the evacuees were carried was often quite considerable. One of the furthest travellers was the famous Roedean Girls School who, after a lengthy journey by rail, alighted on the platform of Keswick Station. On arrival in the Lake District the school took over the Keswick Hotel adjacent to the former Cockermouth, Keswick and Penrith Railway and remained there for four years* ROEDEAN SCHOOL

Maidstone, then to Kings Langley and finally to Bodmin Moor. She writes 'We could never repay the extreme kindness that we were given, with everyone making such a wonderful effort to address the difficulties of my little charges. I was only 21 at the time and did not have much experience of the world at large. When we were moved from Maidstone I was as upset as my little ones, though I will never forget the wonderful treatment displayed by the elderly porter at Kings Langley. When we arrived we had no idea where we were, all the station nameboards were blacked out. The porter looked kindly at the children and said there was no name 'cos of the Jerries, but seen as we didn't look much like parachutists he'd tell us we woz at Kings Langley'. He then gave all the little ones a postcard of the station and told them to write to their mummies and daddies and let them know they were safe on the LMS. He then gave each child a bit of toffee or liquorice stick which he chopped up into small pieces. Later we were moved to the Bodmin area, but the billeting officer did not expect us, so the wives of the railway workers took charge, Boy Scouts were sent around the district and people were asked if they would help to billet us. The new 'uncles and aunties' opened their houses so willingly and spared no thought to their own needs as they tried to make the children part of their family. Everyone was possessed with the same spirit of kindness, the desire to help was overwhelming. Despite all the difficulties of those dark times, we will never forget the way we were received at Kings Langley and in Cornwall. We were deeply and profoundly touched - please express my thanks through your book to all the railway men who, like Jesus advocated, remembered the little children!'

Left: *In order to facilitate the success of the evacuation, the Government began to initiate ways for parents to visit their children more frequently than had hitherto been permitted. The provision of cheap tickets and special trains alleviated a situation which had built up into a major row, when enterprising private bus operators had been prosecuted for running excursions to evacuation areas. On April 18th 1940, parents queue at Paddington for the 9.45am to Reading, Didcot and Oxford and the 10.08 special to Cheltenham, Gloucester and Hereford. Note also the complete absence of children which suggests that this is not normal holiday traffic.*
ATLANTIC COLLECTION

Armoured trains

The fear of a German invasion in either Scotland or East Anglia had prompted the construction of the British armoured trains of World War I in 1914. However, by contrast, no such urgency was put into providing armoured trains in 1939, as the combined British and French navies so significantly outnumbered their German counterpart. It was tactically correct therefore, that far more importance was attached to the nation's air defence systems. Elderly coastal defences, gun emplacements and the forts of major river estuaries were revitalised however, many utilising old pieces of naval ordinance which had been taken off warships scrapped between the wars. Yet, as problems grew in Europe the threat of invasion of Britain looked increasingly likely, War Minister, Anthony Eden, turned his attention to protecting Britain from Operation Sealion - the German code name for the invasion. Simultaneously the Home Command, began to requisition more of the former naval guns in store, as well as purchasing a number of weapons from ordnance depots in the USA.

Giving mobility to these weapons was something else, as the available tanks were mostly just equipped with machine guns, and therefore useless in an anti-tank role. Accordingly, Lt. Colonel Alan H. Mount, the Chief Inspecting Officer of Railways suggested that armoured trains be formed for service in Kent, Sussex, Devon, Cornwall and up the east coast from East Anglia to the north of Scotland. In May 1940, a meeting was held at King's Cross Locomotive Depot with Sir Nigel Gresley, William Stanier, Lt. Colonel Mount and Captain Cantlie of the Transportation Department at the War Office, when the plans for the make up of armoured trains was decided upon. The LMS took on responsibility for providing the train, comprised of two armoured trucks and two low-sided wagons, whilst the LNER would provide the motive power. For the twelve trains that had been ordered by the War Office, Gresley chose the ex-Great Eastern 2-4-2 tanks designed by Wordsell in 1894. Eleven of these were Class F4s (built between 1906-09) and used on the suburban services from Fenchurch Street and Liverpool Street, the other was a class F5, No.7784 (built 1904). Stanier used the new LMS 20-ton all steel coal wagon, which was modified by having a cut down front (to allow a field of fire) and 'armoured' by fitting an external skin of 3/16th" steel plate, and an internal skin of

Following the demonstrable success with armoured trains during the Boer War, the War Office asked the Railway Executive Committee to consider how best such trains might be employed in a defensive role for Britain. On November 14th 1914 a sub-committee of the Executive authorised the construction of two armoured trains for coastal defence. Each train consisted of: two 30-ton Caledonian Railway boiler trolleys, converted for use as gun trucks; two 40-ton GWR coal trucks, which were covered and used as infantry vans; and an 0-6-2 side tank locomotive. Later a tender was provided to allow extra range for running long patrol routes on the NBR north of Edinburgh and the Midland & Great Northern Joint Railway in East Anglia. All the vehicles were fitted with protective skirts to prevent hand-grenades being tossed beneath the wheels.

BRITISH RAILWAYS EASTERN REGION, AUTHOR'S COLLECTION.

1/4" mild steel. The spaces between the skins and the original wagon sides was filled with a 4 inch layer of concrete. The wagons were then fitted with Mark II 6lb 6cwt Hotchkiss guns. The two supply trucks for each train were modified 3-plank dropside wagons of a 1935 design. Work progressed quickly on both locomotives and the vehicles, so that the first train was delivered to the coastal artillery school at Shoeburyness on June 21st 1940.

Tests with the armoured train showed that the shortened gun could be trained dead ahead without fouling any vehicle which might be attached to the train, whilst at the same time traversed to either side without fouling the loading gauge. Significantly, it could also be fired whilst standing free on the rails, thus avoiding the time consuming process of screwing the vehicle down. Unfortunately, the only ammunition available was armour-piercing shot, so the gun's theoretical full range of six miles could not be tested. Even so training began in earnest, with the armoured trains being manned by two separate branches of the army. For train crewing the Royal Engineers Railway Detachment supplied the men (many of whom had just been repatriated from France), but the duties of manning the armoured train itself fell to the Royal Tank Regiment. Initially, just two officers and two NCOs from each train were sent to Shoeburyness, for they would then train the other ranks when the allocations of men and trains were assigned to their operating bases. All twelve trains were in readiness by July, and the allocations began. Six were earmarked for the Eastern Command, and six for Scotland - following on the principle of where the armoured trains were most needed

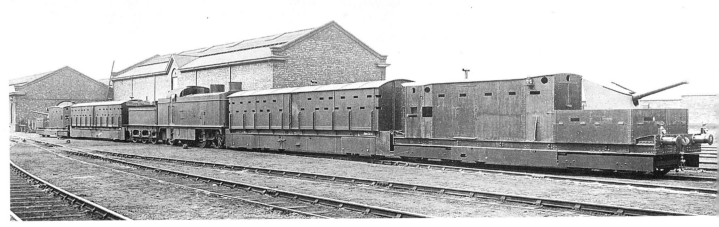

On March 11th 1940, the War Office declared a large part of Northern Scotland a protected area, including the Far Northern Section of the former Highland Railway and the line to the Kyle of Lochalsh. Because the Inner and Outer Hebrides were also protected, the line to Mallaig was also given extra military protection. Six armoured trains were allocated to Scotland, although on the route north the locomotive for Train 'I' broke down at Aisgill Summit on the Settle & Carlisle Railway. Train 'K' was initially stationed at Edinburgh, but soon moved to Longniddry due to operating problems. Trains 'B', 'H' and 'M' were transferred to Northern command in July 1940 as a consequence Train 'K' had its patrol routes extended, with destinations such as Glencorse, Gorebridge, Inverkeithing, Leadburn, Linlithgow, Peebles, Penicuick, Reston and St. Boswells. This May 1941 shows Train 'K' at an unidentified location during one of its patrols.
COURTESY, POLISH INSTITUTE AND SIKORSKI MUSEUM

in World War One. Of the Eastern Command trains, four were used in East Anglia and two in Kent. The Scottish Command quickly began to establish a country-wide patrol in view of the sparsely populated terrain, but one wonders why the units were used on seemingly secure stretches of coast line like that through Ayrshire.

It had been hoped that as many as 20 trains would be built, but the orders for the remaining eight were rescinded and the Northern and Southern Commands began to clamour for their own trains. In fact, the Southern Command proposed working in collaboration with the Royal Navy for armoured trains mounting heavier guns. The War Office acted quickly, and the trains were redistributed so that each command had units at its disposal. Why the desire for armoured trains was so strong may, or may not, have had anything to do with their tactical value. True they could reach parts of the coast road vehicles could not, and they could also offer fire power that the available tanks did not have; yet, in considering all of the facts, it seems likely that the area commanders favoured the trains so highly because they were

probably one of the few heavy combat units which the home command could count on keeping, despite the crises and military shortages that might arise in foreign theatres of war. Needless to say, it was not very common for the armoured trains to cross the command

boundaries which resulted in situations like that evidenced at Sutton Bridge where the trains of Eastern and Northern Commands met at a rather isolated spot on the old M&GNR. Some commanders took the training of their armoured train crews very seriously, as for

One of the few British Generals who immediately recognised the value of armoured trains, Lieutenant General H. R. Alexander (pictured with the cane) is seen with Armoured Train F at Newton Abbot Station in April 1941. To his right, alongside the engine is Colonel Michalski, the Polish officer who did such stirling work in bringing these coastal defence units up to an acceptable standard.
COURTESY, POLISH INSTITUTE AND SIKORSKI MUSEUM

One of the benefits of the armoured trains was their flexibility, easily being moved from location to location, but whilst ever the support crews were located in static positions, the effectiveness of the units was rather questionable. To overcome this problem a number of Continental ferry vans, which had been stranded in Britain, were employed as stores van. Later a number of coaches were obtained to expand the accommodation for the support units. One such coach, an ex-North Eastern clerestory composite is seen with a ferry van at Manningtree, Essex in April 1942.
COURTESY, POLISH INSTITUTE AND SIKORSKI MUSEUM

An undated view of Armoured Train G, but taken after May 1941, as the train is equipped with one of the ex-Caledonian Railway bogie tenders which had been armour-plated and provided to increase the train's patrol range. The location is also unrecorded, but is more than likely in East Anglia. At first Train 'G' worked the Hunstanton - Kings Lynn line, and the associated branches to places like Wells-next-the-Sea, but from September 1941 began covering most of the lines as far south as the Thetford - Cambridge route.
COURTESY, POLISH INSTITUTE AND SIKORSKI MUSEUM

example did Major Dransfield of No. 1 Armoured Train Group. In August 1940 he borrowed a bomber and crew from the RAF to reconnoitre the patrol route of Train G between Kings Lynn and Wells. For good measure he also organised a mock bombing raid on the

train 'to keep the men on their toes.'

Down in the West Country the three trains transferred to the Southern Command began to patrol most of the secondary lines in Devon and Cornwall. It was of particular concern to the officer commanding the South West, Lt. General Alexander, that the Germans might make an attack on the river estuaries which bit deep into both the northern and southern coasts of the isthmus. A successful raid by a relatively small force could easily have cut off the slender road and rail links, providing the enemy with a toe-hold in Cornwall which it would be difficult to remove them from. Of particular concern was the Camel estuary, so the line between Wadebridge and Padstow became a major patrol route. Another danger point, the Fowey River was less easy to patrol due to stabling difficulties, but at least once a week the Wadebridge train made an extended trip on the GWR line through Bodmin, Lostwithiel, Fowey, Par and St. Blazey to Newquay. In Devon Train A was ready for action up the Teign Estuary or between Brixham and Kingswear, whilst Train F was up at Barnstaple, running regularly between Ilfracombe and Torrington.

Around the end of August the threat of invasion was at its height, and the train crews prepared for the almost inevitable codeword "Cromwell", which would signal that an invasion was imminent. On the night of Saturday September 7th, the word came and the crews went to readiness, around 11pm the crew of Train J believed they had witnessed the start of the hostilities when the church bells of Stirling ran out - the warning that parachutists had landed. By 2.15am the Police had reported that

the warning had been given in error, but the train steamed out on its patrols for a further 12 hours. By the end of September it was clear that the invasion would not come that year and that Hitler had changed tactics. Much needed breathing space was given to the various home commanders, and preparations began in earnest for the coming spring and summer. As far as the trains were concerned it was evident that the extensive running was taking a toll on the locomotives, and occassionally one of them would be out of service for repair, at which times the patrols were not operated or an un-armoured locomotive was drafted in. This saw SR Class C and 01, LNER F3 class and various GWR 0-6-0s being drafted in as temporary replacements, so four more armoured engines were ordered as spares for delivery in January of 1941. At the end of 1940 orders were also placed for armoured tenders to carry extra water and coal to increase the range of the patrols, but deliveries did not take place until the following summer, meanwhile Train F at Barnstaple was fitted with a searchlight as an experiment.

During 1941, much of the patrol pattern was the same as the previous autumn, but things were beginning to change. By this time, the need for tank crews was evident elsewhere, so proposals were made that the Polish army should take over the operation of the armoured trains and thereby relieve the men of the Royal Tank Regiment. Though the Royal Engineers would still man the train operating posts, the Poles were excellent replacements for the combatant duties, having long been conversant with the construction and operation of armoured trains. A feeling in the War Office that the armoured trains were 'Boer War' relics, and a general lack of conviction that the independently minded Poles were any use, seemed to make an ideal way of addressing two unwanted problems by combining them together.

The feeling of smug superiority disappeared as soon as the Polish army began their training with the armoured units, effectively working alongside the Tank Regiment crews until these were withdrawn. Under the command of Colonel Lodzia Michalski the armoured trains were organized into a superb defence force, in fact looking through the War Office records, it rather seems as though the Poles looked down on the improvised British trains as being inferior to their required standards. Whatever, Michalski certainly brought the units well up to standard, providing them with support units including mess-coaches, stores vans, bren carriers and additional armaments including

During the course of the preparation of this book, it was my pleasure to speak with Mr. Robert Gregson of Wadebridge, who had served as a fireman on Armoured Train D when it was allocated to Cornwall. Mr. Gregson had been repatriated from Dunkirk after service with the ROD in France, and was subsequently sent to Shoeburyness to train up for his duties with these units. After his service in Cornwall ended, he was transferred with the train to Manningtree in Essex early in 1942. Shortly afterwards he was sent to Longmoor Military Railway to train as a driver, but his train remained to patrol lines round Ipswich, Harwich and along the north coast of the Thames Estuary. It is pictured by the cattle-dock at Manningtree on March 25th a few weeks after his departure.
COURTESY, POLISH INSTITUTE AND SIKORSKI MUSEUM

two Vickers machine guns for each train.

However, the passive defensive role was not completely suiting the Poles who wanted more active duties, so from the end of 1941 onwards Michalski began indicating that he wished to withdraw his units from armoured train duties- suggesting that they might be replaced by the Home Guard. However, the numbers of Home Guard troops in the remote coastal areas where the trains patrolled posed a serious problem, and only Scotland agreed to take on the responsibility. The Poles therefore continued with the units in East Anglia which would be joined by two from the West Country, but those attached to the Northern Command would be disbanded in April 1942. Concentrating the remaining English units in the south-east of the country may not have been the best tactical deployment of the armoured trains, but administratively it proved to be so. As the threat of invasion receded, the value of the trains as a defence force, in England at least, became less and less. For the Poles and the Home Guard units working alongside, they were more effective for training purposes.

By the beginning of 1943, the home defences were the most secure they had been during the war, whilst the tide of war overseas was also changing in the Allies favour. The armoured trains were redundant, and the troops crewing them were transferred into the 1st Polish Armoured Division which was being formed in advance of the second front opening up. Disbanding in England began in April and was completed by September, but the canny Scots hung on to theirs a little longer - in fact it was not until November 5th 1944 that the War Office notified the Railway Executive that the last of the armoured trains had been disbanded. The engines were returned to the LNER and overhauled at Stafford before going back into anonymous suburban service. However, by 1947 each one of these engines was carrying a little cast plate giving recognition of their war service which read:

DURING THE WAR OF 1939-45
THIS LOCOMOTIVE WAS ARMOURED
AND HAULED DEFENCE TRAINS
ON THE COAST LINES.

D-Day preparations

Before any possibility of opening up a second front could be entertained, there was the need to begin the accumulation of men, materials and equipment which would be required for an offensive on mainland Europe. This meant bringing in overseas aid. Like the civilian ports around the country, those owned by the railways were of considerable value during this build up; for example Newport showed its usefulness in the receipt of incoming aid from America, whilst Stranraer provided a vital bridgehead to the army training grounds in Northern Ireland. A new military port was constructed at Cairnryan, near to Stranraer, in order to handle the extensive levels of traffic crossing the Irish Sea. Further to the north the Clyde estuary became the principle receiving point for American troops, a role which had been played principally by Liverpool in World War I. However, the Clyde was now considered marginally safer from the Luftwaffe than the Mersey. This necessitated the establishment of an organisation called The Clyde Anchorage Emergency Port who, under the auspices of the Ministry of Transport, dealt with the reception and onward transportation of the convoy traffic. Unfortunately, large liners like the two Cunard 'Queens', could not use the quay at Gourock. As these ships brought over whole American divisions at a time, smaller vessels (including a number of Clyde steamers) were used to disembark the troops and their equipment in mid-channel. They would then be taken over to the quayside stations at Gourock and Princess Pier, where Railway Transport Officers moved them as expeditiously as possible to the training camps. Simultaneous to the inward receipt of troops and equipment, the LMS and LNER also handled a large amount of traffic which was leaving the Clyde for the far east.

Whilst the Mersey, Bristol Channel and Clyde ports all had a major part in the reception of the convoys carrying overseas aid, pride of place as far as the D-day invasion forces go, belongs to the ports served by the Southern Railway; including Dover, Folkestone, Littlehampton, New Haven, Plymouth, Portsmouth and, of course, Southampton. In preparation for the great flow of rail traffic which would be routed to these ports in the summer of 1944, railway links from the north were substantially improved, a task which included the complete doubling of 18 miles of single track on the Didcot, Newbury & Southampton Junction line. Other lines were also improved in connection with this work, including the provision of spurs between the GWR and Southern lines at Launceston, Lydford and Yeovill. These spurs facilitated an important flow of traffic towards the southern ports, particularly those in the West Country where almost every river estuary, inlet, and bay was packed with landing craft 'awaiting orders'. Since it was planned to land 130,000 men in Normandy on the first day of the operation, followed by further waves of new troops as beach heads became established, it was essential that the lines of communication down to the embarkation points were kept clear of obstruction. Train controllers prepared long in advance, devising a system of moving men and equipment which could be contrasted with the modern merry-go-round system of coal movement today. Even lines which remained just single track, such as the important route connecting Stranraer with Dumfries, were kept free from congestion by careful train pathing and the extension of loops and sidings.

The D-Day build up had begun on the railways in March 1944, with somewhere between 9,000 and 12,000 special trains being run up to the middle of June. In the three weeks prior to D-Day this increased to about 3,300 per week, though figures are complicated by the fact that some journeys which crossed company boundaries were counted twice. The railways conveyed around 230,000 men to embarkation points in the period up to August 5th, which, when compared to the overall requirement of 300,000 men is a significant 76% of the total. Other special train movements in the period show 12,000 tons of baggage, 436 tank trains and 817 specials carrying petrol and other fuels. To facilitate this movement, hundreds of lay-back sidings were converted into loops, whilst completely new loops were put in elsewhere. Many of these 'holding loops' were to be of limited use, with a short life expectancy, so they were made in a cost-effective way. Instead of sleepers, the track was mounted on concrete blocks similar to the practice employed by the old Stockton and Darlington Railway. However, whereas the S&DR stone blocks were free standing, the concrete blocks had the benefit of a cross tie rod every third pair. After the war these blocks were extensively used for other purposes; a substantial number came to light recently during the conversion of the Bishop Auckland Viaduct from (rail to road), when the contractors found what they first thought was a solid sub-soil retaining wall.

In the prelude to D-Day the loops and sidings

The receipt of the inward goods from American and the Dominion states, sustained Britain as she prepared for the invasion of Europe, but it placed yet another strain on the railways who had to deal with all the traffic. For example, at the new port of Cairnryan in Scotland, a Military Railway was established to handle the massive level of traffic between Britain and Northern Ireland. The LNER engines are all on loan to the War Department. From left to right, class J50 No.1058, and War Department Nos. 82, 85 and 81 - all Class J69 0-6-0s.

NATIONAL RAILWAY MUSEUM

were packed with long freight trains awaiting the order to move on. Stanier 8Fs, Austerities, S160s and even ROD 2-8-0s of World War I origin were seen, quietly simmering at the head of up to 100 wagons per train. Arthur Penny, a Railway Transport Officer working in south Oxfordshire recalled the sheer number of trains, saying 'it was a good job the Jerry bombers had eased back by then, there were so many columns of smoke going up, places like Witney Junction, Kennington and Didcot could have been seen for miles and miles on a clear day. It was the same at dozens of other major junctions, Bristol, Cheltenham, Guildford, Gloucester, Reading, Salisbury, Swindon and Tonbridge. But once you got down to the likes of Bodmin Road, Chichester, Exeter, Fareham, Petersfield, Three Bridges, Truro, Winchester and Yeovill the columns of trains awaiting movement was beyond belief. On many routes the trains were standing block to block on the running lines as well as in the sidings, just waiting for the codeword that would signal the advance.' They waited and waited - true to form, the delay was the British weather!

In excess of 2,100 American Transportation Corps S160 2-8-0s were constructed, with members of the class being sent to Europe, Russia, China, India and North Africa. In total 796 were consigned to Britain, but eighteen were lost when the ships which carried them as deck cargo were sunk by U Boats. Of the rest, 416 were allocated for use on British railways, the GWR and LNER receiving an allocation of 360 between them, the LMS had about 50 but the Southern could not have had many more than a handful. Three of the class allocated to work in Britain suffered serious boiler explosions, these being No.2403 (Honeybourne), No.2363 (Thurston) and possibly worst of all No.1707 which suffered a firebox collapse inside South Harrow Tunnel. In 1943, No.2339 is seen working a goods train at Reading West Junction.
THE LATE M.W. EARLEY, AUTHOR'S COLLECTION

The S160s not allocated for use in the UK were duly stored, but the problem of accommodating 362 large locos was only resolved by clearing out redundant transfer sidings in South Wales, and at one such location, Penrhos, no less than 152 S160s were stored. The difficulty of storing loaded vans full of supplies was much greater, and almost every spare foot of siding was utilised in southern England from April 1944 onwards. This view, at a Southern yard reflects the magnitude of the traffic with row upon row of U.S. Transportation Corps box vans, and open wagons full of small landing craft.
NATIONAL RAILWAY MUSEUM.

After the first book in this series, Chris Hawkins wrote in about the railways' prewar planning, commenting (by way of example), 'almost every LMS shed had work carried out, if only a lengthened ash pit or an extra water column. By 1944 the Traffic Committee were blithely increasing its block grant for these purposes from £50,000 to £100,000 and beyond'. But to this there may be added a codicil, in that the Ministry of War Transport specified 'Schemes which will not see completion in time for the maximisation of the war effort in 1944 will not gain approval.' Research suggests, that perhaps as far back as the mid-1930s, the Ministry were making preparations for the possibility of war in Europe. In the view left, Fireman W. Streader of Camden Shed loads his tender with coal before starting out on a long cross-country troop-train journey on April 20th 1944. ATLANTIC COLLECTION

The movement of tanks around Britain prior to D-Day was substantial, with consignments being sent to training grounds as soon as they became available. Mr. Whatley of Salisbury recalls that the 152nd Regiment were sent to Lowther Park near Penrith. They received their tanks at nearby Clifton Moor Station (LNER) which, incidentally, was the last place where a battle was fought on English soil in the Jacobite Rebellion of 1745. They arrived at Lowther for training in the autumn of 1942 and spent the entire winter under canvas. Their supplies had to be collected from Penrith Station, 5₁ miles away; rations came once a month in box vans, whilst petrol was received in four-gallon cans carried in ex-Private Owner coal wagons. The same station also served the 49th Royal Tank Regiment training ground at nearby Greystoke. As D-Day approached, the trained units were moved south in readiness for the 'big push'. To illustrate this, our top picture shows Cromwell tanks being unloaded from a train of 'warflats' at Winchester. Tank trains were usually made up of 20 'warflats' or 'warwells', a brake composite coach, and often a full brake luggage van. Loading and unloading tanks from rail wagons was always something of a problem, but the 152nd were fortunate because Clifton Moor station had a simple grass platform. However, in the absence of fixed ramps or mounds, elsewhere this operation became a major problem. Accordingly further developments were made with ramp wagons and, in the bottom picture of an official demonstration at Aldershot, it will be seen how effective the solution was. THE TANK MUSEUM (BOTTOM), NATIONAL RAILWAY MUSEUM (RIGHT)

In the three previous pages we have presented a very brief glimpse at the types of freight traffic that were run in connection with D-Day, but it is a subject which has not been well covered by photographers. Indeed, it is an area in which we would like to find more material. Without adequate illustrations it is impossible to portray an impression of how much traffic the railways moved during the D Day build-up - even the United States Department of Defence has few suitable views in its massive archives in America and Europe. But this movement of men, machines and munitions was phenomenal, so if any reader can assist we would be delighted to hear from them. Meanwhile, two pictures from the National Collection can be used to demonstrate the movement of men at the beginning of June 1944. In the top picture we witness United States servicemen awaiting their embarkation pictured with kit and weapons at Waterloo. It is interesting to note that the foul weather, which held up the invasion, has now broken. As they wait for their train, sun streams in through the glassless roof - the panes having been removed some years previously as part of the air raid precautions. At the same time we must remember that air raids still presented a serious threat, because within one week of the invasion, V1 bombs began falling indiscriminately throughout the south of England, often doing considerably more damage to the railways than the manned bombers had done. In the bottom view, British soldiers board American vessels at the 'LBSCR port' of Newhaven. In the aftermath of D-Day the railways would continue to perform an important service and, in the four weeks following the Normandy landings, 17,500 military specials were run, including 160 which carried captured German prisoners of war to internment camps in the North and West. In addition 113 special trains carried mail for the troops, whilst over 300 ambulance train journeys were made to convey wounded servicemen from the ports to hospitals inland.

BOTH NATIONAL RAILWAY MUSEUM

The Soham disaster

Throughout the war there were constant examples of heroism by railway personnel, ranging from the bravery of stableman Martin who worked in the blazing ruins at York after the Baedeker raids, to the award of the George Cross to Shunter Norman Tunna of the GWR who removed a blazing incendiary from a wagon load of munitions at Birkenhead. However, one incident standing high above the rest was witnessed in the sleeping market town of Soham in Cambridgeshire in the early hours of June 2nd 1944. In the prelude to D-Day, the Railway Executive were handling around 600 Air Force specials each week, as a large quantity of bombs were being carried to bomber bases to be stockpiled for the softening up operation which would precede the actual invasion. One such 'special' was the train involved in the Soham incident, which was hauled by WD Class 2-8-0 No.7337 and operated by the LNER. The train left the Whitemoor Marshalling Yard, March, at 11.40pm the previous evening, hauling a train of 51 wagons; 44 of these contained a mixture of 500lb and 250lb bombs, the other seven carried detonators. The load had been landed at Immingham and was scheduled to reach its destination at the Goodmayes Yard on the GE line at Colchester. However, in view of the sheer volume of traffic, the train was re-routed straight to USAAF airbase receiving station at White Colne in Essex. This involved the train taking an indirect route via Ely, Fordham, Bury St. Edmunds, Ipswich, Colchester and Marks Tey.

At Ely, driver Ben Gimbert and his fireman Jim Nightall took the single line from Dock Junction and headed south east on what, by now, was becoming a routine duty. However, as they approached the end of the 5 miles of single track at Soham, Gimbert saw that flames were coming from the wagon immediately behind the engine. Presumably sulphur dust left behind from previous loads had been ignited by a spark from the locomotive, and the fire had begun to consume straw used as packing for the forty 500lb bombs in the wagon. The train was then doing between 15 and 20mph but Gimbert slowed down, simultaneously sounding his whistle to warn the guard,. Coming to a halt 90 yards from the station, roughly opposite the end of Soham Goods Shed, Nightall descended from the footplate and ran to uncouple the wagon from the train which followed it, inside a minute he was back at the cab reporting his task completed. Gimbert now drew quickly forward, aiming to get the engine and truck clear of the station before it exploded. However, as a diligent railwayman, his concern for his own safety was tempered by his responsibility to others. Knowing that the next section of the route was a double track formation, along which a mail train was due from Newmarket, he slowed down as he passed the signal box to warn the man on duty there. Signalman Bridges came out on to the platform to assure him the next section was clear, but by then the temperature in the wagon had reached a critical point. It was 1.43am.

Forty 500lb bombs exploding in a matter of seconds was an awesome occurrence, and, as may be imagined, a massive force of destructive energy was unleashed on the tiny township. Where the wagon had been a few moments earlier, a crater 15 feet deep and 66 feet wide now stood, whilst the track was destroyed completely over some 40 yards. Signalman Bridges was swept off the platform, the blast which tore apart his box inflicting fatal injuries which would claim his life later that day. The tender of the WD 2-8-0 offered some protection to the crew, but even so Fireman Nightall was killed instantly. The locomotive was pitched over on to its right hand side, but miraculously Ben Gimbert survived. Although grievously wounded and suffering from severe shock, he was later to make a remarkable recovery. Five residents of Soham were seriously injured by the blast, including the station-master who lived in a house alongside the station which was

The selection of views which depict the Soham disaster present the magnitude of the tragedy without elaborate comment. Page 136 shows the Austerity devastated and twisted on to its side against the platform of the tiny station. On the opposite page top, a crane begins to lift the shattered engine, whilst the gaunt remains of the signal box testify to the ferocity of the blast. On the right of the picture, the end wall of the station house will be seen just behind the buffer stop. Finally, the bottom view shows the crater left behind after the explosion, with American army construction units already at work on filling it in. Few passengers of today who pass through the remnants of the tiny station (closed twenty years after the disaster) will ever realise that it was so badly damaged, and yet re-opened for through running inside just 19 hours. AUTHOR'S COLLECTION

razed to the ground. However, the remainder of his family were more fortunate, but nevertheless they were amongst the 22 other people who sustained lesser injuries.

The town was devastated, in addition to the two dead and six seriously injured, there was not a building which had escaped from the damage caused by the explosion or its shock waves. Fourteen houses in addition to the station-master's residence were totally wrecked, with 36 others being rendered uninhabitable. Furthermore, within a half mile radius, a further 700 buildings were affected. Whilst the devastation was extensive, one can only imagine what might have happened had all 51 wagons gone up. Even if Gimbert and Nightall had kept going, the long train would never had cleared the town in time, so the residents of Soham were lucky that such a brave, quick-thinking pair had taken charge of the situation that night. Both men were duly awarded the highest civilian honour for an act of Bravery, the George Cross.

The Home Guard

On May 14th 1940, Anthony Eden, the War Minister, made a broadcast for volunteers to help in the defence of the realm. In his speech he outlined plans for a force made up of men who were not in military service, to carry out part-time patrols and train to assist the army should the country be invaded. The response was massive as old men, boys and those employed in essential work (including railwaymen) enlisted to do their bit. At first the equipment was limited and men were asked to supply their own weapons, and their tactical use against an invasion force in 1940 remains highly dubious. There is little wonder that the Local Defence Volunteers initials were euphemistically changed to Look, Duck and Vanish. Despite the 'Dads Army' concept of the LDV (later the Home Guard), they did play an invaluable role in the protection of civilian installations. For instance they guarded numerous railway lines, including important junctions, stations, coastal lines and major tunnels in order to protect them from possible sabotage.

A plethora of amusing railway stories have been recounted by former Home Guard members, with the result that we have far too many to mention. One account was related by a member of the Honley Home Guard in the Holme Valley of West Yorkshire, who's unit had to invade the neighbouring village of Brockholes on a dark winter weekend in the middle of the war. As will be imagined, with Brockholes Home Guard having to defend their village, rivalry was high. The Brockholes platoon was keen and made up of a number of young men who had not yet been called up for military service, along with a number of 'exempt' engineers who worked at a nearby tractor factory. The force quickly sealed all means of entering the village, by setting up armed blockades positioned over every single road and footpath. A brigadier witnessed their preparations and commended the officer for his thoroughness. However, no sooner than the accolade had been given the Honley Home Guard were swarming all over the village. On capturing the Brockholes HQ, the startled officer asked "How the hell did you get here? We thought not even a mouse could have got through". "Oh", said the elderly officer from Honley, "It was raining so we caught the train".

Another incident was recalled by a Home Guard Unit just a few miles away on the moors above Standedge Tunnel, where the main LMS trans-Pennine line connected Lancashire and Yorkshire. In the early days of the war this tunnel was considered so vitally important that a detachment of 30 regular troops were sent to guard it, including the air shafts high on the moors (down which it was thought that saboteurs might drop a grenade). As the war progressed the guard duties were devolved down to reservists and finally on to Home Guard units from Marsden and Greenfield. Late in December 1941 a heavy raid took place on Manchester, with a number of railway installations including Victoria Station being badly damaged. A stick of bombs were dumped on the moors near Woodhead, but it was initially thought that this was an attack on the tunnel there. Tensions, as might be expected, were running high - particularly so when area HQ reported that parachutes had been seen opening above Mossley and Saddleworth - were the Germans attacking the tunnel? Up on the dark misty moors the youngsters and old men waited tensely until one guard heard a noise approaching him in the fog. His challenge was ignored and no password repeated, so the young man lifted up his rifle and pointed it in the direction of the sound. Suddenly a pair of eyes appeared, glowing in the mist. Again there was no reply to the challenge. The young man took aim and carefully let off the only bullet he had for his rifle, hitting the enemy squarely between the eyes. The platoon dined well on mutton stew for the rest of the week!

A typical military guard duty on railway property, although pictured with a regular soldier on the route out of King's Cross, this was the type of mind-numbingly boring duty that many part-time soldiers were later ordered to perform. One wonders if non-railway enthusiasts would have ever imagined that 50 years on, many of us would pay a small fortune to have been able to capture the sights and sounds, such as the Class V2, that were just part of another duty to them.
ATLANTIC COLLECTION

Demobilisation

When the fighting in Europe ceased on May 8th 1945, the country began to relax. Although the 'forgotten army' was still fighting the Japanese, this was on the opposite side of the world and it did not affect life on the 'home front' as greatly as the conflict with Germany had done. Life started getting back to normal, even though the war in the east was forecast to continue for many months yet. However, just 9 weeks after the end of hostilities in Europe, the world's first experimental atomic bomb was exploded in the New Mexico Desert. On August 6th 1945 a similar nuclear device was dropped on the Japanese city of Hiroshima, followed by a second bomb over Nagasaki three days later - the Japanese Government surrendered within five days.

Perhaps it will come as a surprise to many to read that even though the war was over, the number of troop and military specials continued at a high level for several years to come. For example, in evidence given by the LMS to the Railway Charges Consultative Committee in 1946, it was revealed that this company was still running around 550 troop trains and 300 military freights each week. This high level of traffic on the LMS was, in part, connected with the large number of American troops which were being repatriated back to the States. From camps all over Britain, American G.I.s were being sent to ports such as Liverpool and the Clyde, accompanied by millions of tons of equipment and baggage. A veritable flow of traffic saw an average of 163 'Yankee specials'

As the postwar austerity period took its toll, the railways entered a downward spiral as nationalisation loomed. In many ways, the beneficial social changes that were being brought about in Health and Welfare (such as the Beveridge proposals) did not extend to the nation's transport system. When the physical framework of the economy, the transport infrastructure, was given such a low priority it is little wonder that the nationalised railways were in a desperate state within just a few short years. Compared with the state of the the railways in postwar France, Holland and Germany by 1949 - this view of St. Margarets shed's ex-LNER Class J37 No.64636 at Inverkeithing in 1949 looks positively antiquated as it heads a leave train comprised of a variety of stock. Little wonder that railway travel held little appeal to postwar Britons.

COURTESY M. ELTHAM COLLECTION

being routed north of Crewe - an average of nearly one train every hour. This level of traffic was representative of what was experienced on the other three companies. For example, Southampton, Bristol, Newport all handled exceptionally high traffic flows - including many G.I. brides leaving Europe for a new home 'stateside'. The cross-channel ports were exceptionally busy as might be expected, carrying a two way flow of military traffic for several years. Weymouth concentrated on the transportation of much needed supplies for the newly liberated Channel Islands, whilst Penzance witnessed a number of sailings carrying repatriated German POWs who had been engaged on agricultural work in the West Country.

In some ways the demobilization was very similar to World War I (see pages 58-60), with large numbers of men being held at de-mob centres awaiting their release from military service. A particular feature of the time was the extended leave periods that were granted, with

some stations handling massive numbers of servicemen. At Calne in Wiltshire, 2,749 travel warrants were presented during the Christmas holidays of 1945. Meanwhile, it was essential for the men leaving the forces to be supplied with the accoutrements essential for civilian life, so hundreds of trains were run around the country from the main garment manufacturing centres such as Leeds and Manchester. The exceptional quantity of garments that were despatched is staggering to comprehend, for example between April 1945 and March 1946, the LMS goods agent in Blackpool received and distributed no less than 121,436 'clothing parcels'. A high quantity of returned 'khaki' was also handled by the railway, taking redundant uniforms from demob centres for onward transmission to be shredded and reconstituted in the woollen shoddy mills of Yorkshire. In all, this movement of men, equipment, and supplies assumed massive proportions, in many ways equal to the high levels of traffic averaged throughout the war.

The final analysis

With the declaration of peace, it seemed that at long last normality could be restored and postwar reconstruction begun. However, despite the wish for a better future, a period of considerable austerity began. Bread was rationed, something which had not been seen in Britain even at the height of U-boat activity. As bread remains the stable fuel for man, so too is coal for locomotives and in this regard the railways suffered as badly as the man in the street when prices increased and quality dropped. Coal which was being delivered to the engine sheds was of an atrocious quality, resulting in consumption rising by the staggering figure of over 10lbs per mile on average, an increase in excess of 25%. Fuel became a major consideration throughout 1946, no-one could understand where it was going and why it was so expensive. Commercial operations which relied extensively on supplies of good coal, such as the railways and power generators, anxiously looked towards oil as being a possible alternative. Unfortunately, despite plans to convert a number of coal-burning locomotives to oil (including no less than twenty GWR 2-8-0s), a sufficient supply could not be guaranteed and the scheme was finally discontinued in 1948. The concerns over fuel supplies were exacerbated by the exceptionally severe winter of 1946-7, when terrible weather swept the country from end to end.

The lack of oil supplies is, perhaps, another factor in why little consideration was given to the growing trend of modernisation on American railways where diesel traction was fast supplanting steam. Excellent plans for experimental diesel systems were rejected almost out of hand, including a plan for an East Coast Main Line fleet for use by the LNER. There is little wonder, then, that as the postwar era continued, the LNER and Southern were more than anxious to pursue their prewar railway electrification schemes - but even these were to feel the stringent constraints of the postwar period of austerity. In some ways it is quite understandable that priorities in the latter half of the 1940s were directed towards addressing the damage war had wrecked on the towns and cities of Europe. In Britain this obviously included the supply of good housing, which saw plans for numerous 'housing estate' building programmes, temporary prefabricated homes and extensive repair schemes for houses destroyed or damaged in the blitz. Even prior to the end of the war, the railways had been storing bricks, slates and other items salvaged from bomb sites on behalf of the Ministry of Supply. These stores, along with new materials, were now to be transported by the railways to the construction sites. Traffic from the brickworks like Peterborough and stone, sand, slate and gravel quarries around the country was strictly controlled, with wagon flows being regulated so that they could be unloaded and returned promptly in order that production could be maintained at the quarries etc.

Yet, despite the continuing flow of civilian and military traffic, coupled with that connected with Postwar Reconstruction, the railways continued to struggle on without much needed resources. To many it seemed that the Government was deliberately ignoring the condition of the railways, despite the fact that they had been the life-blood of the nation for the past six years. Few travellers realised how much of a beating the track, locomotives and rolling stock had taken in the six years of hostilities - and how much of a beating they would continue to take until money was provided to address the arrears of maintenance which had built up. Track maintenance alone was something like 45% below target nationally, the same was true of locomotives - many of which were well beyond the end of their projected lives. This is not to say that any part of the system had deteriorated below acceptable safety limits, but far too much of it was right on the very borderline. In addition to these much needed repairs, equipment replacement was desperately needed along with

Getting back to normal, seen shortly after VE day GWR 4-6-0 No.2921 arrives at Oxford with a semi-fast working on May 21st. Note, however, the grimy condition of both locomotive and stock and detectible wear to the permanent way.
CROWN COPYRIGHT, AUTHOR'S COLLECTION

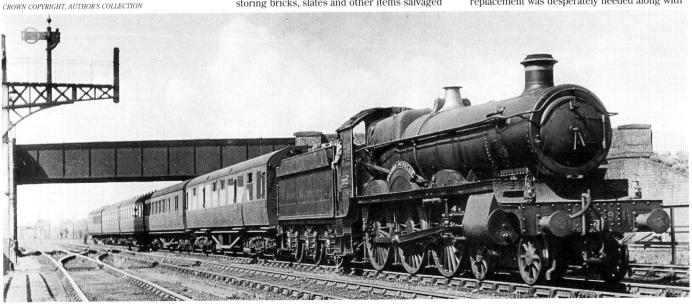

The atrocious winter of 1947 is something worth recalling! In what is now the Peak District National Park, trains were blocked up for days. Most dramatically affected was the line from Buxton to Ashbourne and the Cromford & High Peak Railway. Anyone who has walked over the trackbed of these lines in recent times will appreciate how it became possible for no less than four locomotives to get snowbound at Hindlow Quarry. In this view, an ex-MR 4F on snow-plough duties battles its way through a cutting where the drifts are higher than the locomotive.
R. LEACH COLLECTION.

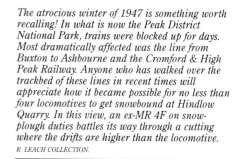

new infrastructure works. One far reaching report considered that following the war commuter traffic in and out of London would increase, with passengers being willing to travel much greater distances. In 1946, a report put forward proposals for a series of new underground lines which would take the main railways across the capital. One such example, would have seen through running between Paddington, Charring Cross and Waterloo. In fact, no matter how well these schemes could have organised the railways for postwar reconstruction they were never implemented due to the severe financial considerations of the day. It is with great regret that the transportation infrastructure changes that could have been achieved in the rebuilding of our bomb damaged cities were not given a fair chance, never would such an opportunity for reconstruction come about again. However, even money for war damage was at a premium and priorities had to be attached to the long list of railway works awaiting attention. Similarly, routine maintenance was held up far longer than it ought to have been. This unwillingness to spend money resulted in a score of serious, but preventable, high speed derailments after track failed at different points around the country in the five years following the war. Interestingly, some of the repair work that was undertaken was to benefit from war-time technology, such as prefabricated track sections with concrete sleepers and the use of mechanical diggers/excavators. In human terms, the war also took its toll on railway personnel, with men in all grades of work taking sick leave or early retirement - a situation which caused a severe strain on the railway convalescent homes and union sick pay funds. This strain was not just limited to the workforce, because many managers were worn out by the time the hostilities ended. Similar to the premature demise of C. J. Bowen Cooke of the LNWR shortly after the end of World War I, October 12th 1945 saw the death of C. E. Fairburn, CME of the LMS, at the relatively young age of 58.

To provide a bit of light relief, we might mention that from June 1945 onwards, the railways carried many people on their first holiday in years. Ironically, many went to stay at former military bases which had been turned from army camps into holiday camps. Perhaps the greatest exponent of what we might call the 'Hi-de-hi' concept was Billy Butlin. Up at Pwhllheli in North Wales and at Filey on the Yorkshire coast, new stations were built to cater for the incoming summer visitors at the Butlin

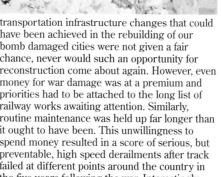

The ambitious nature of the LNER's postwar planning was perhaps most significant of all the Big Four companies, and with the benefit of hindsight we can see it contrasted strongly with the Government's attitude and the resulting standstill on new works. By perpetuating the control of the Railway Executive committee, it stifled initiative and created uncertainty so that many principle express services never returned to their prewar standards. A major problem during this period was a lack of good steam coal, and as a result services were badly affected by poor time-keeping. Some eight minutes behind schedule, a Glasgow (Queen Street) - Edinburgh express waits to leave Cowlairs Junction behind Class B1 No.1217 on August 22nd 1947.
COURTESY M. ELTHAM COLLECTION

camps. Perhaps one effect of the postwar period which was increased by the urge to 'get away from it all', was a 'baby bulge' which lasted between 1946 and 1954. As a product of that era, I was a small contributory part of the increase in home-making, which in turn resulted in new families making significant demands for clothing, furnishings, carpets and furniture - much of which was still on ration. The railways, despite their battered and bruised state were still expected to carry all this additional traffic, yet at the same time they were continually denied the funding which had been promised under the terms instituted when the State took control of the railways in 1939.

It is not without good suspicion, that many postwar commentators believed that a plan for the railways to be taken fully into public ownership at the earliest opportunity had already been devised in the minds of senior civil servants. As early as November 1945 the Labour Party announced that it was their intention to nationalise the railways and introduce the legislation during the life of the first post-war Parliament. Opposition was at once formed against the nationalisation schemes and the four Chairmen in the Railway Companies Association began a fight against the proposals. In this they found an unusual ally in the shape of the Road Haulage Association who were also facing nationalisation into the proposed British Road Services organisation. A more sensible plan was put forward by a group of junior railway managers, which proposed that the Government just take control of the infrastructure (shades of Railtrack). At the same time this would still allow the Big Four to continue to operate services as private operators on a nationally owned system but the idea was actually rejected by the Railway Companies Association. Instead each of the Big Four continued to fight for independence, and at the same time press for proper war service compensation. However, the fight was almost defeated from the start as the Atlee Government began steam-rolling a massive programme of social and economic change through Parliament. The scheduling with which the Bills went through the House was achieved with a precision which a railway pathing expert would have been proud.

The Act which achieved the railway nationalisation, was granted Royal Ascent on August 6th 1947, with the vesting to be the first day of 1948. The Government announced that British Transport Commission would be comprised of Chairman, Sir Cyril Hurcomb

After six years of war, the nation was ready to relax any way it could, despite the austerity period and the bleak winters which had been experienced. Throughout the land people began flocking to the seaside and the countryside, imposing a large burden on the railways which were struggling to carry ordinary traffic. In the summer of 1948, the Southern Region prepares to handle the visiting traffic with a trio of class R1 0-6-0Ts. In the first summer of nationalisation Folkestone shed's Nos. 1128 and 31340 are joined by No.1339 from Canterbury West - this visitor is readily identifiable by its cut-down boiler mountings and shortened chimney, as one of the class altered for service on the Canterbury and Whitstable branch. COURTESY M. ELTHAM COLLECTION

However, not all was doom and gloom on the railways in postwar Britain, as a number of new express services were introduced. Of these, the first new named train to be introduced by British Railways left Bradford Exchange at 10am on May 31st 1948. The introduction of the South Yorkshireman restored a popular prewar Bradford - Marylebone service, which had been suspended in September 1939. This was a service that had existed in various forms since the opening of the Great Central, and its resumption was warmly welcomed as part of the improvement in services by the new British Transport Commission. NATIONAL RAILWAY MUSEUM.

Designed for war, but productive in peace. After the cessation of hostilities, a large number of Austerity and 8F 2-8-0s were released from service with the ROD and allocated on loan to the Railway Executive Committee. Initially running with 7XXXX numbers, they were later renumbered 9XXXX As this class was so useful, they were widely employed on all regions of British Railways, though the 2-10-0s worked mainly in Scotland after an initial allocation of a small number to depots in Carlisle. On June 2nd 1949, a war locomotive was captured on film by E.D. Brunton as it earned its peaceful employment carrying potatoes from Bodmin Moor to London, via Dawlish in Devon contrast with Isaiah 2:4.

(former Permanent Secretary at the Ministry of Transport) and Lord Ashfield (Chairman of London Transport) John Benstead (former General Secretary of the National Union of Railwaymen), Lord Rushmore (former General Secretary of the Co-operative Union), and Sir W. V. Wood (of the LMS). The railway arm of the commission was to remain the Railway Executive, now comprised of Sir Eustace Missenden (Southern Railway) W. P. Allen (ASLEF), V. M. Barrington-Ward (LNER), D. Blee (GWR) J.C.L. Train (LNER), General Sir W. J. Slim and, as natural choice for position of Chief Mechanical Engineer, R.A. Riddles, who had returned to the LMS from the Ministry of Supply in 1943. A small staff was appointed, and took up residence in attic rooms over the London Passenger Transport Board offices in Ealing Broadway. Although the Executive eventually occupied two floors in the building and had a full time staff of 152, the start, to say the best was most inauspicious - Sir Ronald Matthews of the LNER called it amateurish.

So, the war had taken its ultimate toll and at midnight on December 31st 1947 the Big Four railway companies went out of existence. Hardly a thought was given to the people who had made Britain's railways the envy of the world, the investors. For one hundred and twenty-two years these railway company shareholders had speculated, and frequently lost, huge sums of money (often life savings) in financing railway expansion and consolidation. Two periods of war had seen the level of return from the railways diminish considerably, and it was perhaps difficult to expect the private companies to pick ʰemselves up again after World War II, at least ᵗ without substantial Government assistance.

ᵗʰe fifty years on there is much documentary ᵗⁱⁿce to show where it all went wrong, too ᵗᵒ contain in these few brief pages.

Ironically, as I write this book, massive changes once again face our railways with the coming privatising of British Rail. Writing these words and looking out of my study window as a privately owned steam special charter train pounds past on the Settle & Carlisle Railway, it seems we have almost come full circle. Sadly, the railways that are up for sale today are but a shadow of what they were on August 4th 1914 and they will never be the same again. Since that fateful day eight decades ago much has changed, mostly for the worst, despite great technical advances. Throughout the war years, the railways and the men and women who worked on them acquitted themselves with distinction. Working long arduous hours they proved it was not just a 'cushy' number to dodge the bullets. As a slogan of the day announced - 'the railways carried on'. Yet after it was all over, people in the railway industry began to feel bitter, there is no wonder! The bitterness grew to outright hostility after the Conservative Government commissioned Dr. Richard Beeching's infamous report *The Reshaping of British Railways* which recommended massive closures. The decimation of the railways in the Beeching era, just twenty years after the end of World War II, was one of the most heinous

crimes ever carried out by a Government against its transport system. Continual erosion of lines and services was witnessed through the 'seventies and 'eighties and, coupled with privatisation in the 1990s, the scandalous treatment of the British railway network has been just too much for many old railwaymen to bear. Most of those who saw service in the war years will never regret their contribution to the nation's survival, but few can be proud of what has happened since. In the future, the people who will operate our railways will probably be hard-headed businessmen who care little about the sort of service that endeared rail travellers back in Edwardian England prior to 1914 - maybe that really was the **Year The World Went Mad!**

Above: *At the end, after it was all over, there was home. Thousands of returning soldiers passed through Britain's main* *line stations on their way to de-mob centres. For this group walking down the sun-lit platform of King's Cross station,* *one era has drawn to an end and another is ready to begin.*

Atla